the
WHIM-WHAM
book

Frogs Autograph Albums
Ghosties Jump Rope Kissing Games Love
Magic Squares Teases Good and Bad Luck Games
Summer Camp Songs Abracadabra Knock Knocks
Minute Mysteries Riddles Cheers Elephants
Tongue Twisters Puzzles
Wishes Mother Nature
The Man in the Moon
The Tooth
Fairy

FOUR WINDS PRESS NEW YORK

contributed by
youngsters, college
students, mothers
and aunts and uncles
from San Jose, California, to
Fort Lauderdale, Florida, and
from Yarmouth, Maine,
to San Antonio, Texas.

the
WHIM-WHAM
book

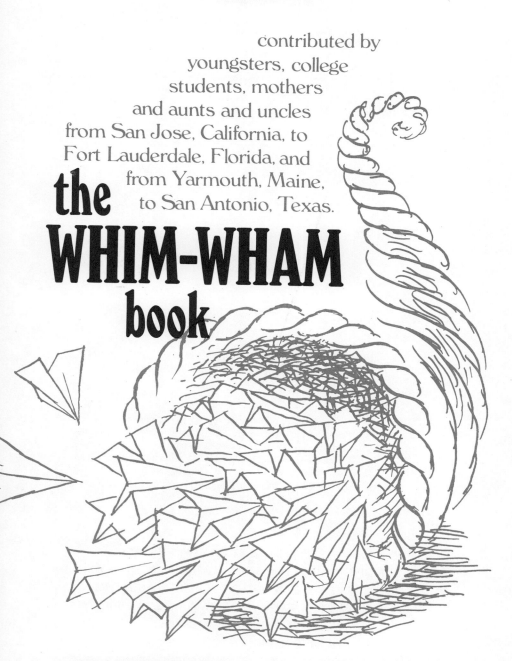

collected by **DUNCAN EMRICH**   illustrated by **IB OHLSSON**

LIBRARY OF CONGRESS CATALOGING IN PUBLICATION DATA

Main entry under title:

The Whim-wham book.

Bibliography: p.
SUMMARY: A collection of riddles, jokes, jump rope rhymes, wishes, summer camp songs, and other Americana alive in the United States today.

1. Folk-lore—United States—Juvenile literature. 2. Wit and humor, Juvenile. 3. Folk-lore of children. [1. Folklore—United States. 2. Wit and humor] I. Emrich, Duncan. II. Ohlsson, Ib.
GR105.W48   818'.008   75-9872
ISBN 0-590-07315-X

PUBLISHED BY FOUR WINDS PRESS
A DIVISION OF SCHOLASTIC MAGAZINES, INC., NEW YORK, N.Y.
TEXT COPYRIGHT © 1975 BY DUNCAN EMRICH
ILLUSTRATIONS COPYRIGHT © 1975 BY IB OHLSSON
ALL RIGHTS RESERVED
PRINTED IN THE UNITED STATES OF AMERICA
LIBRARY OF CONGRESS CATALOG CARD NUMBER: 75-9872
1 2 3 4 5   79 78 77 76 75

The Nonsense Book
The Hodgepodge Book
The Book of Wishes and Wishmaking
The Folklore of Love and Courtship
The Folklore of Weddings and Marriage
Folklore on the American Land
American Folk Poetry: An Anthology

CONTENTS

Don't sail away with this book!

 Debbie Hatcher, McLean, Virginia,
from a book owned by her mother

If I should chance to lose this book,
And you should chance to find it,
Remember that *Judy* is the name
And *Deutsch* that comes behind it!

 Judy Deutsch, Syosset, New York

the
WHIM-WHAM
book

WHIM-WHAM

If you are eating a peanut butter sandwich or drinking a glass of milk, and very obviously doing nothing else, and someone asks you what you are doing, reply: "I'm making a whim-wham for a goose's bridle." A fine non-sensical answer to a silly question!

🌿 Traditional New England

And an equally nonsensical answer given to me by Cynthia Barnett, a student of mine at American University from Illinois:

When you have fallen down and are lying on the floor and someone comes along and asks you what you are doing down on the floor, reply quite simply and clearly and with all seriousness: "I'm teaching the ants their ABCs."

And still another, when it's quite apparent that you're reading or writing a letter. "What are you doing?" "I'm sewing buttons on ice cream."

🌿 Barbara Zeller, Hillside, New Jersey

🖋 This is the third.

🖋 The first book was THE NONSENSE BOOK. The second was THE HODGEPODGE BOOK. NONSENSE was full of riddles, rhymes, conundrums, tongue-twisters, puzzles, and jokes. HODGEPODGE had some of them also, but more about superstitions, customs, beliefs, and folklore about the weather, dogs and cats, bugs, special days of the year, and such.

🖋 This WHIM-WHAM BOOK has some of the same type of material found in both NONSENSE and HODGEPODGE, but with this difference: with one or two exceptions (notably "Magic Squares" and SATOR), everything here comes from youngsters around the country who have written to me; from their mothers or aunts and uncles or schoolteachers; or from my students at American University in Washington, D.C., who come from all over the place—Connecticut, Maine,

Long Island, Maryland, Virginia, Texas, Illinois, and many other states. Which means simply this: that everything in this book is alive and kicking around our country today—in your schoolyard at recess, on your street, in your home or a friend's home.

🐦 When you read WHIM-WHAM, you will find things that you know and also things that you don't. But do this as you read: think of the many things which are almost like what you are reading, or which, if you had been helping me, you would have asked to have included in WHIM-WHAM. Take "Wishes," for example—how do you make a wish? Take "Summer Camp Songs"—you must know half a dozen at least that are not here.

🐦 So, while you read and have fun reading (and using some of the items—"Minute Mysteries," for example), have more fun by adding your own games and rhymes and beliefs to those you find here. Because folklore consists not only of the many things that have been handed down to you from your mother and grandmother and many people long before them, too, but also of the rhymes and jingles and songs and stories that you make up yourself each day. These are items of folklore that you are bringing into being and that will be passed on to your classmates—and they will pass them on to others. Right? Just take "Nicknames," for example. You and your friends make them up for each other all year long. They are as fresh as a daisy. They are folklore—and folklore today. When you read through WHIM-WHAM—and even NONSENSE and HODGEPODGE—you will find your mother's folklore and your own also. Have fun with both.

🐦 Always have fun!

RIDDLES,
Frogs,
ghosts,
Elephants,
and
knock
knocks

6

RIDDLES AND RIDDLE JOKES

What do you see when the smog lifts in Los Angeles?
> *UCLA*

Who has a neck and no head,
Two arms and no hands?
> *A shirt.*

What has feet and legs and nothing else?
> *Stockings.*

What has a stone on its head and a finger in its mouth?
> *A ring.*

What can you give away and still keep?
> *A cold.*

How much is the moon worth?
> *A dollar, because it has four quarters.*

Why is an alligator so deceitful?
> *Because he takes you in with an open face.*

In Tchad—in Africa—they say that the German ambassador was eaten by an alligator: at least he never came back from swimming in the Chari River. This was some time ago.

What has ears but cannot hear?
> *Corn.*

What has four eyes,
    goes out to sea,
        but can't see?
        The Mississippi River.

What did the boy say to the octopus he was dating?
> *I want to hold your hand, hand, hand, hand, hand, hand, hand, hand.*

What is the best way to raise carrots?
> *Grab the tops and pull.*

What's deaf, dumb, and blind, and always tells the truth?
> *A mirror.*

What did one elevator say to the other elevator?
> *I think I'm coming down with something.*

What goes 99, thump, 99, thump, 99, thump, 99, thump . . . . ?
> *A centipede with a wooden leg.*

> 🌿 All from Irv Epstein, Oceanside, New York.

What is the best way to keep a skunk from smelling?
> *Hold his nose.*

What goes "z–z–z–B, z–z–z–B"?
> *A bee flying backward.*

What starts with T, is filled with T, and ends with T?
> *A teapot.*

What were Tarzan's last words?
> *Who greased the grapevine?*

How do you catch squirrels?
> *Hide in the grass and act like a nut.*

> 🌿 Martrice Green, who heard these at the Madison Elementary School, Washington, D.C., in the early 1960s

Where does Lone Ranger take his trash?
> *To the dump, to the dump, to the dump, dump, dump. To the dump, to the dump, to the dump, dump, dump.*

Your teacher will sing you the tune if you don't know it.

> 🌿 Sharon Nash, Washington, D.C.

What did the momma chimney say to the baby chimney?

You're too young to smoke.

What did one chimp say to the other chimp?

Stop monkeying around.

What word when you say it, breaks it?

QUIET! or SILENCE!

🐛 Ginny Eiselman, Bethesda, Maryland

Why did Batman run up the tree?

He wanted to see if Robin had laid an egg.

🐛 Andrew Huston, age 5, who brought it home from school, Seneca, Maryland

Do you know the difference between a tomato and an elephant?

No.

Remind me never to send you to the supermarket.

🐛 Collected by Karen Cohn, Flushing, New York, from Jan Steuber, Wantagh, New York

10

Carrots are good for your eyes.
  How do you know?
Have you ever seen a rabbit wearing glasses?

> 🐸 Collected by Karen Cohn from Marilyn Mayer, Pine Beach, New Jersey

What is this? A deaf man heard what a dumb man said: that a blind man had seen a running rabbit, and that a lame man pursued it, and that a naked man had put it in his pocket and brought it home.
  A lie.

> 🐸 From Karen Cohn's grandmother, Brooklyn, New York

Do you want to hear a clean joke?
  A pig took a bath.

Do you want to hear a dirty joke?
  A white horse fell in the mud.

How do you catch a rabbit?
  Hide in the bushes and make sounds like a carrot.

> 🐸 Caryn Clayman, Bethesda, Maryland, who learned them from eight-year-olds

II

What would we have if all the cars in the nation were pink?
> *A pink carnation.*

> 🌸 Virginia Miller, Washington, D.C.

1st Person: **Why did the rooster cross the road**
2nd Person: **Don't know.**
1st Person: **To get a Chinese newspaper. Do you get it?**
2nd Person: **No.**
1st Person: **Neither do I, I get the *Evening Star-News.***

> 🌸 Sophie Brawner, Chevy Chase, Maryland, collected by Sandy Bell, Washington, D.C.

What's a giraffe after it's seven years old?
> *Eight years old.*

> 🌸 Peggy Stone, Cresskill, New Jersey, from her cousin, Ellen

If Washington went to Washington to wash his wash, how many w's in all?
> *None at all in all.*

> 🌸 Peggy Stone, Cresskill, New Jersey

What do you call a 2,000 pound gorilla?
> *Sir.*

Where does a 2,000 pound gorilla sleep?
> *Anywhere he wants to.*

> 🌸 Marilyn Swesnik, Chevy Chase, Maryland

12

What does LbPb stand for?
A pound of lead.

🐸 Mike Richman, Fair Lawn, New Jersey

What did the Lone Ranger say to his horse?
"Hi Ho Ag" (Hi Ho Silver!)

🐸 Nancy Volz, Smithtown, New York, and learned in her highschool chemistry class, Hauppauga, New York

What did the grass say to the dirt?
Be still. I've got you covered.

Why does a spider spin a web?
Because he can't knit.

🐸 Linda Coleman, Washington, D.C.

What did the fork say to the spoon?
Who is that sharp guy next to you?

🐸 Janice Atlee, age 11, Charles County, Maryland

Why doesn't a vampire bite sleeping people?
He doesn't want tired blood.

🐸 Terry Atlee, age 10, Charles County, Maryland

"Baa, Baa, Black Sheep,
Have you any wool?"
"What do you think I've got—
Feathers?"

    🖎 Sharon Ladenheim, Stamford, Connecticut

What are the three most used words in school?
    I don't know.

    🖎 Janice Hart, age 11, Washington, D.C. The above three riddles were collected from the children by Nahja Smith, Washington, D.C.

Who can speak in all languages?
    An echo.

    🖎 Martha Gollop, Merrick, New York

What man always finds things dull?
    A knife sharpener.

If a green stone fell into the Red Sea, what would happen?
    It would sink.

She: **Hey, how did you get that big gash in your forehead?**
He: **I bit myself.**
She: **Come on, how could you bite yourself on the forehead?**
He: **I stood on a chair.**

    🖎 Phil Paccione, Croton-on-Hudson, New York, who had them from his sister, Gracie Paccione

If two is a company and three is a crowd, what are four and five?

> *Nine. (Fooled you, didn't I? You were trying to think of something complicated.)*

🌺 Rhonda Lustig, Yonkers, New York

If a feather weighs 2 ounces, and a half a box of feathers weighs 1 pound, how much will 2 pounds of feathers weigh?

Try that one on some unsuspecting youngster. It's in the same league as: What was the color of George Washington's white horse?

🌺 Collected by Susan Niemiera from Gene Kaczmarek, Perth Amboy, New Jersey

What goes "Ha-ha-ha . . . CLUNK?"
or
What goes "Giggle, giggle, giggle . . . THUD?"

> *A man laughing his head off.*

🌺 Kate Hayes, Alexandria, Virginia

What goes up when the rain comes down?
An umbrella.

What comes up to the door but can't come in?
The steps.

If April showers bring May flowers, what do May flowers bring?
Pilgrims.

Every time you stand up, what do you lose?
Your lap.

What did the pig cry when the man grabbed his tail?
That's the end of me!

🎋 Margie Kovens Fisher, Bethesda, Maryland, collected from her young niece, Connie Goodman

What do you never say on an airplane?
Hi Jack!

🎋 Linda Ross, from her sister in Belmar, New Jersey

What's the best way to talk to a monster?
Long distance.

🎋 Wendy Sacks, Newton Centre, Massachusetts

Why is a palm tree like a calendar?
Both give dates.

🎋 Phil Paccione, Croton-on-Hudson, New York

How many sides does a barrel have?
Two, an outside and an inside!

🌺 Arlene Eisenberg, Flushing, New York

What has six legs, is green, and hangs from the ceiling?
A grasshopper. I lied about the ceiling!

🌺 Andrea Weiss, Clearwater, Florida, who heard it from Neal Esserman, Arlington, Virginia

What room has no walls
 has no doors
 has no windows
 and has no floor?
A mushroom!

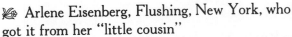

🌺 Arlene Eisenberg, Flushing, New York, who got it from her "little cousin"

Elizabeth, Betty, Betsy, and Bess.
They all went together to seek a bird's nest.
They found a bird's nest with five eggs in.
They all took one,
And left four in.
   How could this be?
One girl: Elizabeth, with three nicknames.

🌺 Beth Barton, Clarks Green, Pennsylvania

What is a honeymoon salad?
Lettuce alone!

🖎 Martrice Green, Washington, D.C.

1st Person: If I had a thousand men and you had a thousand men and we had a battle, who would win?
2nd Person: Me.
1st Person: No, guess again.
2nd Person: You.
1st Person: No, guess again.
2nd Person: I give up.
1st Person: I'd win, 'cause you gave up!

🖎 Victoria Schaeffer, Wyomissing, Pennsylvania, from an 8-year-old, Ari Gold, in Washington, D.C.

1st Person: Did you hear about the terrible accident on the highway?
2nd Person: No, what happened?
1st Person: A big moving truck hit a henway.
2nd Person: What's a henway?
1st Person: Oh, about six pounds.

🖎 Judy Deutsch, Syosset, New York

What four letters of the alphabet would frighten a thief?
O I C U

Why did Santa Claus use only seven reindeer this year?
He left Comet at home to clean the sink.

🖎 Martrice Green, Washington, D.C.

18

What has a head and a tail, but does not have a body?
A coin!

What do you always take off last before you get into bed?
You take your feet off the floor!

🦋 Arlene Eisenberg, Flushing, New York

Why shouldn't you tell secrets in a horse stable?
Because horses carry tales.

What would you have if a bird got caught in your lawn mower?
Shredded tweet.

🦋 John C. Scott, Arlington, Virginia

IMPOSSIBLE, NONSENSE RIDDLES

And you can make these up by yourself by the hundreds. People will think you're crazy, but then possibly you are.

What's the difference between a duck?
What size shoe do you wear? *Brown?*
What color is your hair? *Long?*

    ✎ Marcia Buchwalter, Fairfax Station, Virginia

How high's the water?
Up to the knees on the ducks.

Do snakes have teeth?
That depends on whether they walk to school or carry their lunch.

    ✎ Ellen Fincke, Harrington Park, New Jersey

GHOSTS

What does a ghost eat for dinner in an Italian restaurant?
> *Spookghetti.*

What does a ghost eat for breakfast?
> *Ghost-Toasties.*

What does a ghost say when he's on guard duty?
> *Who ghost there?*

What does a ghost like best to do at an amusement park?
> *Ride the roller-ghoster.*

Why do ghosts like Greyhound buses?
> *Because they go from Ghost to Ghost.*

> 🍃 Martrice Green, who heard these ghosties at the Madison Elementary School, Washington, D.C., in the early 1960s

Big Ghost: Us big ghosts are going to a party and we're going to sing songs.
Little Ghost: What are you going to sing?
Big Ghost: A haunting we will go, a haunting we will go, Hi ho, the scary-O, a haunting we will go.

> 🍃 Courtney Hoover, Chevy Chase, Maryland

FROG RIDDLE JOKES

What does an antique frog say?
Relic, Relic.

What does an automated frog say?
Robot, Robot,

> 🖉 Denise Graham and Lou Ortenzio, Hyatts-
> ville, Maryland, and reported by Jim Baxter
> who said that "frog jokes were very popular
> for a time at my highschool, Northwestern."

WHAT'S GREEN?

What's green and plays the guitar?
Elvis Parsley.

What's green, is skinny, and teaches dancing?
Fred Asparagus.

> 🖉 Mary Ellen Hughes, The American Na-
> tional Red Cross, Washington, D.C.

WAITER!

Waiter! Call me a cab.
All right, sir. You're a cab.

Waiter, do you serve crabs here?
Yes, sir, we serve anyone.

> 🖉 John Meillon, Sydney, Australia. I would
> guess that young John is about twelve or thir-
> teen years old. Very nice of him to send those
> all the way across the Pacific to us!

MORE ELEPHANT JOKES

Why did the elephant wear green sneakers?
> *So no one would notice him when he tiptoed across the pool table.*

Why did the elephant wear one blue, one red, one green, and one yellow sneaker?
> *So no one would notice him in the bag of M & M's.*

Why do elephants like peanuts?
> *They save the plastic wrappers for valuable prizes.*

How can you tell if there's been an elephant in your refrigerator?
> *You can see his footprints in the butter.*

> 🐌 George Muschamp, Arlington, Virginia, the first collected from Mike Gavor, the second from Rick Worssam, and the third from Bill Smith, all of Reston, Virginia

Why did the elephant jump out of the tree?
> *He didn't jump. The hippopotamus pushed him.*

Why do elephants lie on their back?
> *To trip up low flying birds.*

> 🐌 Paul Dengrove, New Brunswick, New Jersey

What do you find between elephants' toes?
Slow running natives.

How can you tell when an elephant is in your house?
His tricycle is parked outside.

Why did the elephant wear red sneakers?
Because his white ones were dirty.

🖋 Helen Metaxas, Margate, New Jersey, and Karen Coburn, Queens, New York

What did the elephant say when he saw General de Gaulle coming over the hill?
Nothing. Elephants don't speak French.

How can you tell a boy elephant from a girl elephant?
The one with the red Keds is a girl.

🖋 Erica Loewenthal, New York City

What do you get when you cross an elephant with a peanut butter sandwich?
You get an elephant that sticks to the roof of your mouth or a peanut butter sandwich that never forgets.

🖋 George Muschamp, who learned it from Kevin Davis, Reston, Virginia

How do you shoot a blue elephant?
With a blue elephant gun.

How do you shoot a pink elephant?
Hold his nose until he turns blue, and then shoot him with a blue elephant gun.

🖋 Jo Anne Kessler, Brooklyn, New York

24

KNOCK KNOCKS

Knock, knock.
Who's there?
Canoe.
Canoe who?
Canoe come out and play with me?

Knock, knock.
Who's there?
Madame.
Madame who?
Madame foot's caught in the door.

Margo MacGregor, River Vale, New Jersey

Knock, knock.
Who's there?
Sam and Janet.
Sam and Janet who?
Sam and Janet evening . . . (to be sung)

Nancy Gendler, South Hampstead, New
York, and heard from friends at camp, Monroe,
New York

Will you remember me a year from now?
Yes.
Will you remember me six months from now?
Yes.
Will you remember me a month from now?
Yes.
Will you remember me a week from now?
Yes.
Will you remember me a day from now?
Yes.
Will you remember me an hour from now?
Yes.
Knock, knock.
Who's there?
I thought you said you'd remember me!

  ✍ Peggy Stone, Cresskill, New Jersey

Knock, knock.
Who's there?
Atch.
Atch who?
Gesundheit.

  ✍ Collected by Karen Cohn, Flushing, New
York, from Barbara Friedman, Montclair, New
Jersey

Knock, knock.
Who's there?
Morris.
Morris who?
Morris Monday, next day's Tuesday.

Knock, knock.
Who's there?
Boo!
Boo who?
Don't cry!

Knock, knock.
Who's there?
Arthur.
Arthur who?
Arthur any more at home like you?

🦋 All three from Jeannette Paroly, West
Orange, New Jersey

Knock, knock.
Who's there?
Howie.
Howie who?
I'm fine, how are you?

🦋 Helen Metaxas, Margate, New Jersey, and
Karen Coburn, Queens, New York

Knock, knock.
Who's there?
Della.
Della who?
Delicatessen.

Knock, knock.
Who's there?
Marcella.
Marcella who?
Marcella's full of water and I'm drowning.
Help!

    🌸 Erica Loewenthal, New York City

Knock, knock.
Who's there?
Olive.
Olive who?
Olive you.

Knock, knock.
Who's there?
I see.
I see who?
I see you!

    🌸 Susan Blumenfeld, Oceanside, New York

Knock, knock.
Who's there?
Sarah.
Sarah who?
Sarah doctor in the house?

    🌸 Nancy Van Alstine, Bethesda, Maryland

Good and Bad Luck

GOOD AND BAD LUCK

You can believe these if you want to, partic-ularly the good luck ones. Some people don't believe any, but then they're missing a lot. Ready?

If you sing while you are walking upstairs and you don't finish the song by the top of the staircase, you will have bad luck. (Moral: Sing quickly or walk slowly.)

> Collected by Audrey Lee, River Edge, New Jersey, from Mrs. Billie Botti, Long Island, New York

When you go over railroad tracks in a car, pick your feet up or you will have bad luck.

> Andrea Brown, Washington, D.C.

If the initials in your name spell a word, it is bad luck.
If your name has thirteen letters, it is bad luck.
If it has seven letters, good luck.

> Helen Metaxas, Margate, New Jersey and Karen Coburn, Queens, New York

When my grandmother was a little girl and played hopscotch, if she could find a piece of red glass to play with, it was GOOD luck, and she would win.

    🌺 Tamlyn Perry, Yarmouth, Maine

If you see three nuns riding in a car, it is very good luck.

    🌺 Margaret Trytell, New York City

It is bad luck to play cards near a church.

    🌺 James Moulder, Haverford, Pennsylvania

When someone is not expecting it, slap their arm and say "Got you last!" The person who is slapped will have bad luck all day.

    🌺 Doris Indyke, from elementary school friends, Rockville Center, New York

It is good luck to hang a branch of the first crop of cherries over your bed. Doing this means that you are bringing into your home a fresh breath of Spring or the first juices of Spring.

    🌺 Eve Wright, Garrison, New York

If you tie your shoes by accident with three loops for the bow instead of the usual two, you will have good luck.

    🌺 Mary Balicki, Chicopee, Massachusetts

32

HORSESHOES

Jane McAuliffe of Glencoe, Illinois, **says very simply that "horseshoes bring good luck." Quite true.**

Eve Wright of Garrison, New York, **goes her one better, however, by pointing out that "to find a horseshoe is a lucky omen. It is regarded as a good luck omen because it resembles the crescent moon." The crescent moon is the new moon, the growing moon, and I suppose that any wish that you make on the horse- shoe—after you spit on it and throw it over your left shoulder—will come true as the moon grows.**

Now Cathy Robertson of Oyster Bay, New York, **offers very sound advice which is generally believed everywhere. "When you hang a horseshoe above your door to bring you luck, always nail it with the open end up. If you nail it with the open end down, all the luck in it will run out and it will no longer be of any good-luck use to you." If you know someone who has mistakenly hung the horseshoe with the open end down, do him a favor by telling him the way it should properly be nailed.**

SILVER DOLLARS

They are now very, very hard to come by. But if you have one or if someone gives you one, hang on to it. Here is a belief about what to do with one: Sleep with a silver dollar under your mattress and you will have good luck.

    🌿 Carol Greenbaum, Jericho, New York

RABBITS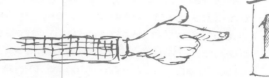

If you say "Rabbit, Rabbit" on the first day of a month as soon as you wake up and before you have said anything else, you will have good luck throughout the whole month.

    🌿 Maggie Miles, from her mother-in-law in New England

"Our version of 'Rabbit, Rabbit' was: If the last words you spoke on the last night of the month were 'Rabbit, Rabbit' and the first words you spoke the next morning (the first day of that month) were 'Bunny, Bunny,' you would have good luck that whole month."

    🌿 Mary Campbell, Chevy Chase, Maryland, who practiced this in high school and even when she was a student at Smith College in Northampton, Massachusetts. You have to remember the last words and the first words: it takes a little bit of doing.

34

Sandy Bell of Washington, D.C., says that on the first day of every month, before you do or say anything, say "Rabbit, Rabbit." If you do, you will have good luck. You should also walk backward down the nearest stairs in order to insure your good luck for the entire month.

A DRINK OF WATER FOR GOOD LUCK

This has nothing to do with "Rabbits," but on the first day of every month, fill your mouth with water, turn around, and walk down a flight of stairs backward. You must also keep your eyes closed tight. Upon reaching the bottom of the stairs, you swallow the water, open your eyes, turn around, and kiss the first person you see! (Who? Who? That's your problem. It could be the milkman, the postman, the boy next door, or your aunt and uncle together. You really do have problems.)

🦌 Eve Wright, Garrison, New York, and learned and practiced at boarding school, Northfield, Massachusetts

A U.S. MAIL OR A UNITED PARCEL SERVICE (UPS) TRUCK

"When I was a little girl someone told me that I would have good luck if I crossed my fingers whenever I saw a U.S. mail truck or a UPS truck and didn't uncross my fingers until I saw another. For years I did this, and I guess I've been pretty lucky."

🖌 Carolyn Peace, Melville, New York

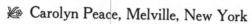

CEMETERIES: HOLDING YOUR BREATH, RABBITS, AND BUTTONS

Holding Your Breath

When you pass a graveyard, hold your breath, because it is not polite to breathe in front of people who can't.

🖌 Maureen Mintz, Camp Woodstock, New York

If you hold your breath when you drive past a cemetery, you won't die tomorrow.

🖌 E. Neil Norris, Greenwich, Connecticut, and now of Washington, D.C.

Hold your breath and cross your fingers when passing a graveyard in order to secure a long life.

🌿 Megan Holbrook, New York

Hold your breath while passing a cemetery, or someone you love will be the next to be buried there.

🌿 Peter Weidlein, Mt. Kisco, New York. He says also: "I had to pass a very large cemetery every day."

When you drive past a cemetery, it's good luck to hold your breath.

🌿 M. Patricia Egan, Villanova, Pennsylvania

When passing a cemetery, you must hold your breath until you have passed it. If you fail to do this, harm will come to a member of your family. This was particularly difficult when passing an unusually long cemetery in Brooklyn, New York.

🌿 Lindsay Dane, Franklin Square, New York

Rabbits

These rabbits have nothing to do with the first-of-the-month rabbits, which are quite different. These are cemetery rabbits.

When you pass a cemetery, say "Bunny, bunny, bunny . . . ." After you have passed the graveyard, finish by saying "Rabbit." This will help you hop over the burial grounds.

🌿 Deborah Rodock, Canton, Ohio

When you drive past a cemetery, say "Bunny bunny, bunny . . ." until you come to a white house. Then say "Rabbit" to avoid bad luck.

🐚 Amy Singer, Barrington, Rhode Island

When passing a graveyard, say "Rabbit, rabbit, rabbit," and it will bring you good luck.

🐚 Maureen Mintz, Camp Woodstock, New York

Whenever you pass a cemetery a common custom is to hold your thumbs up and say "Bunny, bunny, bunny" until you completely pass the cemetery, and then turn your thumbs down and say "Rabbit."

🐚 Judy Deutsch, Syosset, New York

When you pass a cemetery, you should always point your thumbs up—indicating that you want to go in the direction of Heaven.

🐚 Madeline Lefkowitz, Paramus, New Jersey

Buttons

My sister and I always hold onto a button while passing a cemetery.

    🐚 Belle Fingold, Highland Park, Illinois

Always hold onto a button when you pass a cemetery. If you don't have a button, hold your breath.

    🐚 Nancy Gendler, South Hampstead, New York

The Cemetery Itself

If you walk across a person's grave, your toes will rot.

    🐚 Elizabeth Miller, Pittsburgh, Pennsylvania

And you all know, of course, that when you suddenly shiver for no reason, someone is walking over your future grave or a rabbit is running across it.

When you sneeze in a cemetery or talk about death (either in the cemetery or out of it), always pull your ear lobes down.

    🐚 Robert Orr, Washington, D.C.

Shake a Piece of Cloth

When you pass a cemetery or when you are passed by a funeral procession, always shake a piece of your clothing (skirt, shirt, blouse, necktie) to keep the spirit of death away.

    🐚 Brenda Lebowitz, New Rochelle, New York

SLIPS (GIRLS') GOOD AND BAD

If you put your slip on backward in the morning, it is bad luck to turn it around.

> 🐚 Doris Indyke, Rockville Center, New York, who learned this from her grandmother

If you put your slip on inside out, it's bad luck to change it.

> 🐚 Cynthia Barnett, Decatur, Illinois

If someone unintentionally puts on a garment inside out, it's good luck. (Baseball players believe this: socks, sweat shirts. And if they believe it, and if you want the Orioles and Yankees and Dodgers to win, you'd better not change your outside-inside clothing until the end of the game or the end of the day. Stick with luck!)

> 🐚 Virginia M. Towsey, Washington, D.C.

PENNIES AND OTHER COINS

If a penny is found heads up, it is good luck. If it is tails up, it is bad luck.

> 🌿 Helen Metaxas, Margate, New Jersey, and Karen Coburn, Queens, New York

If you see a penny on the ground, Pick it up, And you'll have good luck all year 'round.

> 🌿 Penny Tamsen, Newburgh, New York

When you see a penny on the ground and it is tails up, you should not pick it up and keep it. Instead, pick it up and throw it over your right shoulder. Only pennies which are found heads up are lucky.

> 🌿 Judith Warrington, Seaford, Delaware

A flattened penny is a good luck piece to carry when you are traveling.

> 🌿 Mary Balicki, Chicopee, Massachusetts. To flatten a penny, simply place it on a railroad track or trolley-car track, and when the wheels run over it, the penny will be very flat.

If you find a coin (any coin), you should keep it as a lucky piece. If you spend it, you will have bad luck.

> 🌿 Fran Goodman, Mount Vernon, New York

ONE SHOE OFF

For every step that you take with one shoe off and one shoe on, you will have one day of bad luck. (Always best to have both shoes on or to go barefooted: saves you from stumbling in any case.)

  Judith Warrington, from her aunt in Tennessee

A LUCKY STONE

Sometimes you will find these, and when you do, keep them. They are quite rare. A stone with a naturally made hole completely through it is lucky. Usually you will find them by brooks where running water has worn a hole through the stone. You can even thread one on a string or ribbon and wear it around your neck or on your wrist for constant good luck. Have you seen one?

  Irv Epstein, Oceanside, New York

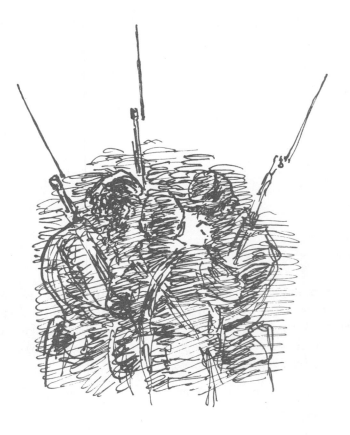

THREE ON A MATCH

Three on a match is, of course, bad luck and known by everybody. But why? Some say it comes from World War II. Not so. It goes way back of that, to the Civil War at least. When soldiers were in the trenches and lighting cigarettes or lighting the fuses for their rifles, an enemy sharpshooter could see the glow of the match. On the first match, he sighted. On the second match, he took careful aim. On the third match, he fired. Three on a match: death. Unlucky, of course.

Jane McAuliffe, Glencoe, Illinois

NEW YEAR'S EVE CALENDAR

On New Year's Eve, take a calendar for the upcoming year. Close your eyes and point to a date. On that day something very good will happen to you. It will be a very lucky day. You can take a calendar that shows the whole year, or a calendar that is broken into twelve pages for the twelve months, or a desk calendar that has 365 separate pages —one for each day. Any calendar will do, but you must choose at random with your eyes closed. And look forward to your LUCKY DAY!

🌺 Doris Indyke, Rockville Center, New York

HONEY APPLE

If you eat an apple dipped in honey (doesn't the thought of it taste good?) on New Year's Eve, you will have a good year.

🌿 Doug Brooks, Brooklyn, New York

IN AND OUT THE SAME DOOR

This is old and very well known: Always go out of a house or apartment by the same door you entered. If you go out by another door, it will bring you bad luck.

🌿 Michael August, Silver Spring, Maryland

SILENCE!

It is bad luck to talk when you are riding over a bridge. (Be quiet and then babble afterwards. You probably didn't have anything really too important to say anyhow, did you? The bridge is the wonderfully important thing.)

🌿 Judith Warrington, from a friend in New York

RED

A red coin (one with red paint on it) must always be placed in a piggy bank first in order to attract more coins.

🐾 Peter J. Skiba, New Jersey

Tie a red bow on a new car for good luck—a small one on the radio antenna or on some gadget on the dashboard.

🐾 Carol Greenbaum, Jericho, New York

Janice Polizzi gets a little more complicated with her new cars. Number one: When you buy a new car, place a pair of scissors with a red ribbon tied around them in the glove compartment for good luck. And number two: When you buy a new car, put a dash of salt and a dash of whiskey in the glove compartment for good luck. Now, if the family had a third car, what would you put in the glove compartment? Give it some thought. Something for good luck.

🐾 Janice Polizzi, Northvale, New Jersey

A DEPARTING VISITOR

It is very bad luck to watch a friend who has been visiting you drive out of sight. Always turn away and go back into the house or about your business before he or she is out of sight. This may mean that if you watch them, you are worried about them, or worried that they won't come to see you again. This is widely believed.

Collected by Larry Kester from Mary Gay Reusel of Rockland, Maine

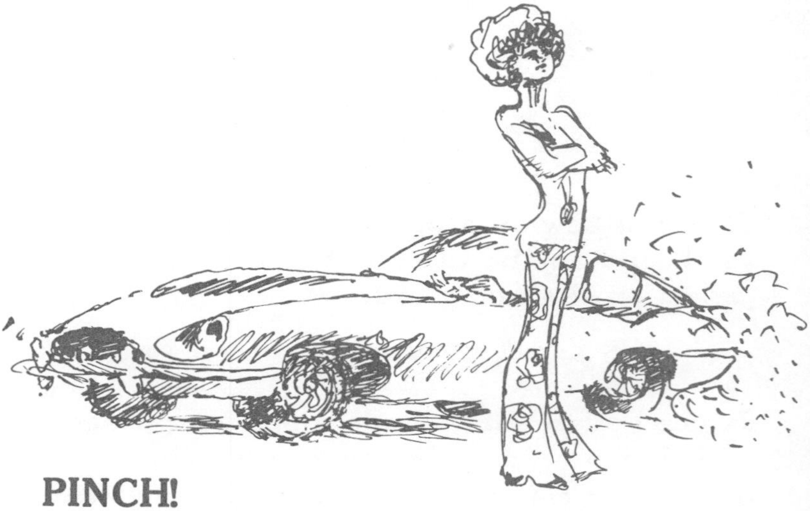

PINCH!

If you are riding in a car and pass a car with an out-of-state license, pinch the person next to you and you will have good luck. (But the person next to you won't, because he or she could be black and blue by the end of the drive—unless he or she very alertly first pinches you! It works both ways, you know.)

Doris Indyke, Rockville Center, New York

RIGHT FOOT

If you are taking a walk, even on your way to
school, and you hit something (a stone, a
tree stump, a rock, or anything) with your
right foot, you will have good luck. If you
hit something with your left foot, you will
have bad luck.

    ✒ Virginia Towsey, Washington, D.C.

If you want to win at a game of cards or
have good luck all day long, put on your right
shoe first in the morning.

    ✒ Judy Deutsch, Syosset, New York

I remember this from somewhere: The left
side of your body is the Devil's side and the
right side is God's side; so people who write
left-handed owe one day's work a year to the
Devil. This is, of course, nonsense since your
body is one and whole and belongs to—guess
Who?

FOURTH FINGER

If someone pinches your fourth finger and you scream, you will have bad luck for a week.

> 🌿 Maggie Miles who heard this from a friend from Arkansas

FRIDAY

It is bad luck to cut your fingernails on Friday. (That is true, of course. Saturday is a much better day, or Sunday, when you can take your time and not hack at them in your rush to get to school.)

> 🌿 Helen Metaxas, Margate, New Jersey, and Karen Coburn, Queens, New York

Friday the 13th. If June the 13th falls on a Friday, it is very good luck, because it is the Feast Day of St. Anthony who performed 13 miracles.

> 🌿 Linda Ross, Belmar, New Jersey

THE IRISH MOUSE

The Irish mouse is a tradition in our family. Each home should have one. The mouse represents good fortune and food-a-plenty because he would not reside in a house with a bare cupboard. If the mouse leaves, the home despairs, and bad times will surely follow.

🐭 Miriam Montag, from her family in Connecticut, but traced back to County Wexford, Ireland, in the 1800s

abracadabra,
Magic Squares,
and
SATOR

52

A MAGIC TRIANGLE: ABRACADABRA

This is really wonderful. And the "magic" of the triangle lies in the fact that you can follow the word Abracadabra many, many ways through the triangle. You can read it across the top; you can follow it down the left side to the bottom and then up the right side to the top; you can start with the first or second (or the first three, or first four) letters on the top line and then drop down to the second line and third line, and then go across and up to the top again on the right; and any number of other ways always beginning on the top left with the letter A.

```
A B R A C A D A B R A
  B R A C A D A B R
    R A C A D A B
      A C A D A
        C A D
          A
```

MAGIC SQUARES OF NUMBERS

In *The Hodgepodge Book* I gave you a simple
magic-number square, and here it is again.
Whichever way you add the numbers, they
always total 15:

4	9	2
3	5	7
8	1	6

Up and down or diagonally, always 15.

Now, here are three more. The first (above)
was three times three. The second below is
four times four. The third is five times five,
and the fourth and last is six times six. Try
them on your math prof, or grandfather.

Four times four, and add them up or down,
across, or diagonally, and the total is 34:

4	14	15	1
9	7	6	12
5	11	10	8
16	2	3	13

54

Five times five:

11	24	7	20	3
4	12	25	8	16
17	5	13	21	9
10	18	1	14	22
23	6	19	2	15

They all total 65, up or down or across, or diagonally.

Now, six times six. And the total here in any one of the directions is 111. These are magic squares, and they may protect you from mumps or whooping cough or an older sister. Who knows?

6	32	3	34	35	1
7	11	27	28	8	30
24	14	16	15	23	19
13	20	22	21	17	18
25	29	10	9	26	12
36	5	33	4	2	31

And even if you don't experience any magic from them, they will give you a very, very good opportunity to test your knowledge of addition. Try adding any of the rows of figures up and down or across—and diagonally. It's quite wonderful the way they work. No? Yes.

THE <u>SATOR</u> MAGIC SQUARE
OR FORMULA

Word squares that can be read in four directions—up, down, left to right, right to left —are rare. But they were considered to have magic powers, protecting the owners from evil, witchcraft, fire, mad dog bites, and such. A simple example of such a square is one made up of two Latin words (Roma and Amor) and two German words (Sarg and Gras). Reading up and down, right and left, you'll find each word four times:

G	R	A	S
R	O	M	A
A	M	O	R
S	A	R	G

But the most incredible magic square of all time is the SATOR square. Follow this closely and then show it to your mother and father, aunt and uncle, and schoolteacher. It will astonish them. Have your schoolteacher read this and then explain it to your class. It's worth knowing. Here is the square. Never mind what the words mean for the moment. They don't make much sense, but we'll get to them shortly.

There are five words, and each one appears four times as the square is read from top to bottom, bottom to top, left to right, and right to left.

Second, print the words out in sentence form:

SATOR   AREPO   TENET   OPERA   ROTAS.

What do you find? You find, first, that the sentence spells backward and forward the same. What next? You find that the first letter of each word spells the first word. And the second letter of each word spells the second word. And the same for the third and fourth and fifth. Now then, start with the last word and repeat the process from back to front. The last letter of each word spells the first word. The next to the last letter of each word spells the second word. And so on throughout.

The words, by the way, are Latin but do not make a good sentence, so don't try to find a sentence in them. The words are *sator,* meaning a "sower" of seeds; *arepo,* meaning "I creep" or "I cease"; *tenet,* is "he holds"; *opera,* is "works"; and *rotas,* are "wheels." It is not the sentence which is important, but the secret magic in the square.

To understand the secrecy of it, you must know a little bit about its history. The square has been found scratched on the walls of buildings which were standing in England during the Roman occupation, on Roman garrison walls in Mesopotamia, on Roman buildings in Gaul (France), and in Italy and Germany. But the most astonishing place where it was found scratched was on a wall in Pompeii—and Pompeii was destroyed by the eruption of Mount Vesuvius in 79 A. D., which makes the square pretty close to two thousand years old! Now, during the days of Rome, the Romans persecuted the early Christians who had to resort to secrecy to identify themselves to each other, and to aid and protect each other.

Take another hard look at the square, and what do you see?

You see the word "tenet"—"He holds"— twice to make the form of a cross. So you have the Christian symbol of the Cross and the words "He holds," meaning "God holds" as a secret means of identification within the square. It had meaning for the early Christians—and there were Christians even among the Roman soldiers—but the square otherwise looked like magic nonsense to anyone not initiated into the secret. Now, one more thing. Notice that by each letter "T" you have the letters "A" and "O," at the top and bottom and on the sides. "A" and "O" in Greek stand for Alpha and Omega, the first and last letters of the alphabet, or in other words, "the beginning and the end." So you have "God holds" and "He is the beginning and the end." Secret Christian words and signs.

You think you're finished with the secrecy and magic?

No.

You come now to the greatest discovery of all about this magic square, and the discovery was made by Felix Grosser of Chemnitz, Germany, in 1926. It is utterly incredible.

What Grosser did was to take the twenty-five letters of the square, put each on a piece of light cardboard, and then shuffle them around on a table top in an effort to find out whether there was any other secret in the square. He didn't really know what he was looking for, but he felt that there must be something else there. There was, and he found it. Twenty-one of the letters formed another cross out of the two Latin words "Pater" (Father) and "Noster" (Our), the first two words of the Lord's Prayer:

```
                    P
                    A
                    T
                    E
                    R
    P A T E R N O S T E R
                    O
                    S
                    T
                    E
                    R
```

Now you have four letters left over, and guess what they are—two Alphas and two Omegas, "the beginning and the end," again.

Place two at the top and two at the bottom, or one at each of the four ends of the cross, and you have three great secrets and symbols of the early persecuted Christians: the cross, the Lord's Prayer, and the everlasting nature of God.

So, the greatest magic square of all time with its secrets.

puzzles and problems

62

YOUR AGE
AND THE CHANGE
IN YOUR POCKET

1. Take your age, and multiply it by two.
2. Add five.
3. Multiply by fifty.
4. Subtract three-hundred-and-sixty-five.
5. Add the loose change in your pocket under a dollar.
6. Add one-hundred-fifteen.
7. The first two figures in the answer are your age, and the last two the change in your pocket.

🌸 Jim Baxter, West Hyattsville, Maryland

For example: Suppose you are ten years old and have fifteen cents in your pocket.

Your age:	10
Times 2:	20
Add 5:	25
Multiply by 50:	1250
Subtract 365:	885
Add the loose change—15 cents:	900
Add 115:	1015

The first two figures are your age (10) and the last two the change in your pocket (15).

EYE, EAR, AND LIP, TOE, LEG, AND ARM

Do you want to bet a nickle or a dime with an aunt or uncle? Ask them to name five parts of the human body above the neck and five parts below the neck, each one of which is spelled with only three letters. And they must do it within a time limit of four minutes. And all the words must be strictly medical terms. No slang is allowed. Here they are:

eye	toe
ear	leg
lip	arm
gum	rib
jaw	hip

They will easily guess the first three in each group, but the last two become much tougher. Try it. But be prepared to pay up if you lose!

🦋 Larry Coffey, Arlington, Virginia

A TRAIN AND ITS PASSENGERS

This is very tricky! A train started out with 20 people. It stopped and let off 2 and picked up 3. It stopped again and picked up 5. It stopped another time and let off 3. At its next stop it picked up 11 and let off the same number. It stopped once more and picked up 2. At its final destination everyone got off. How many stops did the train make?

Everyone whom you question will expect to be asked how many people were on the train, and not how many stops the train made. The train made six stops, counting the last.

🌿 Leslie Fink, North Bellmore, New York

"I CANNOT OPERATE..."

A man and his son were driving in a storm and hit a fallen tree. The man was killed instantly, and the boy was rushed to the hospital for surgery. The doctor came into the operating room and said, "I cannot operate on this boy. He is my son." If the boy was the doctor's son, who was the man in the car?

Answer: The boy's father. The doctor was the boy's mother.

✍ Leslie Fink, North Bellmore, New York

TWO INDIANS

There were two Indians walking down a path, a big Indian and a little Indian. The big Indian was not the little Indian's father, but the little Indian was the big Indian's son. Who was the big Indian?

Answer: The little Indian's mother.

✍ Kristin Pfoutz, Cabin John, Maryland

A BASKET AND FOUR APPLES

There is a basket with four apples in it. There are four girls. How can we divide the apples so that each girl gets a whole apple and one still remains in the basket?

Answer: Give three girls an apple each, and give the fourth girl her apple in the basket. (Sneaky, eh?)

🖎 Fran Goodman at American University who learned it from Louis Dolin, Mount Vernon, New York

MULTIPLICATION

Multiply 1 2 3 4 5 6 7 8 9 by 8, and see what you get!
987654312

It's too bad that it doesn't come out 321, which would make it perfect. But it's pretty good anyhow.

A SINKING SHIP

A young man dreamed that he was on a ship at sea with his father and mother, and that the ship had begun to sink. It was, however, possible to save himself and one other person only—either his father or his mother, but not both. What should he do?
Answer: Wake up.

🌿 Karen Cohn, Flushing, New York

MINUTE MYSTERIES

70

MINUTE MYSTERIES, OR VERY TRICKY PROBLEMS

"Instead of telling ghost stories," Janice Keidel of Arlington, Virginia **says that "a favorite camp activity was to tell 'Minute Mysteries.' These are tricky little stories that must be figured out by the listeners in order to make sense. Otherwise the stories seem strange and weird. To figure them out, you may ask any number of questions of the story-teller but only questions which can be answered by 'yes' or 'no.'"**

1. A man walks into a bar and asks the bartender for a glass of water. The bartender points a gun at the man as if to shoot him. The man says, "Thank you," and walks away. What happened and why?

1a. (A variant from Debra Chaykin, Brooklyn, New York) **A man walked into a drugstore and spoke for a minute with the pharmacist who was behind the counter. The pharmacist then drew a gun and held it on the customer. Why?**

By asking any number of questions answerable by "yes" and "no," you arrive at the solution: The man was suffering from hiccups. The bartender and pharmacist knew that a sure cure for hiccups was fright. Each pulled out a revolver to cure the customer's ailment.

2. A man kissed his wife good-by before going to work, closed his apartment door, walked to the elevator, pushed the button, and knew his wife had died. What happened?

The elevator did not come because the electricity had failed. His wife was sick and had been breathing with an electric heart-lung which stopped when the electricity went off.

3. "I guarantee," said the salesman at the pet shop, "this parrot will repeat every word it hears." The customer bought the bird, but it never spoke a word. What the salesman said, however, was true. How could this be?

The parrot was deaf.

4. A man is found dead in the middle of a field with a pack on his back. There are no cuts or open wounds on him. How was he killed?

He was parachuting, and his parachute did not open.

5. At Sloppy Joe's Restaurant a customer was shocked to see a fly in his coffee. He sent the waiter back for a fresh cup. After his first unthinking sip, he suddenly realized it was the same coffee he had had before. How?

It had cream and sugar in it.

6. A man rides on horseback from New York City to Virginia. The trip normally takes four days. He leaves New York on Wednesday and arrives on the same Wednesday. How could he do this?

His horse is named Wednesday.

🦢 Margie Stegman, collected from her thirteen-year old brother in Norwalk, Connecticut

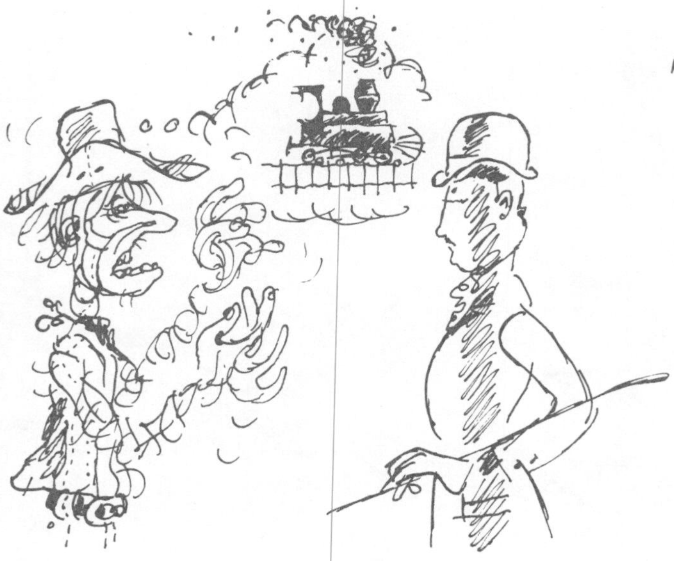

7. A night watchman was in a stable guarding the owner's prize horse. One night he dreamed the horse was run over by a train. He told the owner that it was a sign that something bad would happen to the horse. What did the owner do? He fired the night watchman. Why?

The night watchman was sleeping on the job.

Pam Valente, Kinston, North Carolina

8. A man lives on the 21st floor of an apartment building. Every morning he gets into the elevator, presses the button for the first floor, gets out and goes to work. Every evening when he comes back, he gets in the elevator, pushes the button for the 14th floor, gets out and walks up to the 21st floor. Why does he get out at the 14th floor instead of pushing the button for the 21st floor?

Because he is a midget and can't reach the 21st button. (But you would think that he'd carry a small cane to poke the button with, wouldn't you? I would if I were a midget.)

Karen Nichols, Brooklyn, New York

9. Five men were on an island. One of the men was murdered by one of the other four. The body lay next to a bush where the two had been struggling. The police arrested all four men and said that within twenty-four hours they would know who the murderer was. How?

> *The bush where the two men struggled was poison ivy. Poison ivy has a twenty-four hour incubation period before it shows. At the end of that time, the police would have the murderer.*

🌿 Gary Lerman, Brooklyn, New York

10. A man has hung himself in a large room with a rope extending twenty feet down from the ceiling, but ten feet above the floor. There is nothing in the room except a large puddle of water on the floor. How did he hang himself?

> *He stood on a large cake of ice which melted under him.*

🌿 Also from Gary Lerman

11. A woman was arrested and found guilty of murder. She was sentenced to death, but the execution could never be carried out. Why not?

> *She was a Siamese twin.*

> 🌿 Judy Deutsch, Syosset, New York

12. John and Mary are lying on the floor—dead. There is water and broken glass all over the floor. A black cat is sitting in the corner. What happened?

> *The cat knocked over the fish bowl, and John and Mary are the fish.*

> 🌿 Also from Judy Deutsch

13. A man is walking down the street and sees an albatross hanging in a butcher shop window. He runs into the shop and jumps into the window and takes a bite out of the albatross. Then he runs out of the store and runs down the street shouting, "Thank God, I'm free at last!" What happened?

> *He had been a sailor and had been marooned on an island with shipmates. They were close to starvation, and there was only an albatross to eat. The men drew lots, and one of the men was killed and eaten also. Both the albatross and man were cooked by two volunteers in different pots beyond a small ridge and out of sight of the rest of the sailors. Half the survivors ate the man and half ate the albatross, without knowing which was which. The man wanted to find out which he had eaten, and discovered that he had eaten the albatross.*

✍ David Wildberger, Baltimore, Maryland

14. And one last one, but you can make others up for yourself and probably hear some from friends. A man was found shot to death in a room with 53 bicycles. What happened?

I'll give you a quickie batch of "yes" and "no" questions, but I'll also tell you that it took a class of students four days to come up with the answer after asking innumerable questions. But let's pare the questions down:

Q. Was there anyone else in the room?
A. No.

Q. Had there been someone else in the room?
A. Yes.

Q. What make were the bicycles?
A. That is not a "yes" or "no" question, and I can't answer it.

Q. Were the bicycles two-wheeled?
A. Yes.

Q. Could a child ride on them?
A. No.

Q. Could anyone ride on them?
A. No.

Q. Were they made of metal?
A. No.

Q. Were they picture bicycles on cardboard?
A. Yes.

Q. Were they "Bicycle" brand playing cards?
A. Yes.

Q. But there are only 52 cards in a deck?
A. Yes.

Q. The man who was shot had been cheating and had an extra card, maybe an extra ace?
A. Yes.

> *So you have the solution. Fifty-three Bicycle cards, one man cheating with an extra card, and the person he was playing with drawing a gun and shooting the cheater.*

🖋 Debra Chaykin,
Brooklyn, New York.

GAMES

"SQUIRRELED"

The object of this "game" (if you call it that) is to fool someone into believing something unusual or looking at something imaginary—in other words, getting him to react to nothing at all except what you have made up.

Example 1: "Hey, Joe just got hit with the bat!" (And there probably was no Joe and no bat.)

Example 2: "Mr. Thomas and his doggone tests. You study for it?"
"For what test?"
"The arithmetic test."
"Oh, no!"
"Squirreled you!"

After a successful ruse or trick, you yell "Squirrel" at the friend or classmate or anyone else whom you have suckered into believing you. And watch out, you'll be "squirreled" too.

🐿 Greg Pennell, West Chester, Pennsylvania

MARCO POLO

This is a crazy water "polo" game in a swimming pool with a lot of friends. The person who is "It" is Marco Polo, and he must hunt or search with his eyes closed for any of the others. While he is searching, he screams "Marco." The others all scream back "Polo"—which gives Marco Polo some idea of where they are by the sound. But then, of course, they can move off and change their positions. Whoever is first tagged by Marco Polo then becomes the next Marco Polo.

🐌 Marilyn Swesnik, Chevy Chase, Maryland

THE GREASED WATERMELON

This is another swimming pool game. "A watermelon is greased with vaseline. Then about fifty kids' hands are greased with baby oil. The watermelon is then thrown into the pool. The kids go in also, and the person who can take hold of the watermelon and get it out of the pool owns it. I played this and won!"

🐌 Janet Carney, Trenton, New Jersey

82

THE "GHOST" GAME

This is fun and will test your wits. It can be played while driving in order to pass the time or indoors on a rainy day.

Someone begins the game by naming a state or country that begins with the letter "A." The next person must then name a state or country that begins with the last letter of the word that the preceding person gave. If you cannot think of an answer (and no repeating of a name is allowed), you get a "G," which is the first letter of the word "Ghost." The first person who accumulates enough letters to complete the word "Ghost" loses.

For example:

First person: Arizona
Second person: Alabama
Third person: Afghanistan
Fourth person: Nevada
Fifth person: Arkansas

If there are no more than five playing. it is now the first person's turn again:

First: (she/he can't think of a state or country beginning with "S", so she/he gets the letter "G")
Second: Siam
Third: Missouri
Fourth: India

And so on, everyone slowly accumulating the "Ghost" letters until one is a complete losing Ghost.

🌿 Karen Cohn of Flushing, New York, who learned it from her sister, Bobbi Cohn, about 1965

ANOTHER "GHOST" GAME

The object is to trap a player into completing a word. When the letters named make a complete word, the player who named the last letter earns a "G" for "Ghost," and the game continues until there is a complete losing "Ghost" — g –h –o — and so on. The first person starts with any letter of his choice— for example, T. The second player must add a letter, but always keeping a word in mind. He adds an H, making TH. If the third player should add an E (which makes a word: THE), then he earns the first "G." If he had added an R, then the next player would have had to come up possibly with an I. There's not much choice now for the next player, is there? He's going to have to add an L. And the next player is trapped because he will have to add another L, making the word THRILL. So he earns a "G."

One other rule: If a player adds a letter which seemingly cannot possibly be used in a word, he can be challenged. If he can't come up with a word, he earns a "G." But if he does have a word in mind and can prove it, then the challenger becomes a "G." Wonderful for spelling!

    🖉 Wendy Sacks, Newton Centre, Massachusetts

THE PICNIC GAME

This is a cumulative game. It is played by a group of youngsters or also while driving in a car with your family or friends.

The leader begins: "I'm going on a picnic, and I'm going to take with me an apple."
2nd person: "I'm going on a picnic, and I'm going to take with me an apple and a loaf of bread."
3rd person: "I'm going on a picnic, and I'm going to take with me an apple, a loaf of bread, and some peanut butter."
4th person: I'm going on a picnic, and I'm going to take with me an apple, a loaf of bread, some peanut butter, and some jelly."
And so it goes, each person repeating everything that has gone before and adding a new item each time: pickles, coke, potato salad, cookies, candy, and so on.
You lose and are disqualified if you forget and leave out one of the items being taken on the picnic, or if you do not repeat them in the same order.

🐝 Doris Labie, from her childhood in New York City

HA-HA

"This game was particularly popular around exam time, perhaps because it relieved the strain. It was played just by girls, around 11 to 14 years old.

"Everyone would lie on the floor on their backs. Each girl would put her head on another girl's stomach (like lying on your back with your head on a pillow). You were at right angles with the girl on whose stomach you pillowed your head, and with the girl who pillowed her head on your stomach.

"The first girl would say 'Ha,' the next 'Ha-ha,' the next 'Ha-ha-ha,' and so on until real laughter began. It didn't take long! Soon everyone would begin to laugh, because their heads were being bounced by the laughing stomach they were on. It was against the rules to roll over with your laughter, so you just lay there and laughed until you were exhausted.

"Often just when everyone had stopped laughing, all it took was one girl to start laughing again and bounce the head on her stomach, and everyone who wasn't too weak would be laughing helplessly again."

      Mary Campbell, Chevy Chase, Maryland

SARDINES

This is the opposite of hide-and-seek. One person hides and the rest look for him. When a hunter finds him, he doesn't yell out but hides with him until the last person is left. All are jammed together in the hiding place like a pack of sardines. The first person who found him becomes the one to hide the next time.

🌺 Tim O'Connor, Scarsdale, New York

OWL'S EYES

And you don't have to be very small to play this, although you'll have fun teaching and watching the smaller youngsters.

Owl's Eyes: You play this with one other person. You put your foreheads together so that they are touching and also so that your noses are touching. Your eyes are tightly closed. Then you count to three, you both open your eyes (which are staring bang straight at your friend's eyes), you swivel your heads with your foreheads and noses still touching, and you shout "Whooo—oo—oo!"

> 🥬 Loren Zander, Scarsdale, New York, who reported this said that "Kids love it!"

BUZZ

You can play this in a car to pass the time or indoors with several friends. Start counting from 1 up to 100, each person saying a number. *But* one number has been chosen —say 7—and every time the number 7, or any multiple of it, or any number with 7 in it comes up, the person on whom that number falls must say "Buzz!" instead of the number. Otherwise he is out of the game. *For example:*
1, 2, 3, 4, 5, 6, Buzz, 8, 9, 10, 11, 12, 13, Buzz, 15, 16, Buzz, 18, 19, 20, Buzz, 22, 23, 24, 25, 26, Buzz, Buzz, 29, 30 . . . and so on. Use any number from 3 to 9 for your "Buzz" number. It's good for your arithmetic and will keep you on your toes. The faster the game goes, the more fun it is.

> 🥬 Abbie Casper, Overbrook Hills, Pennsylvania

FARMYARD CHORUS

Suggest this joke-game to a group of players
and, automatically, you become the leader.
(Be sure that there are some players who do
not know the game.) Then, as leader, you
whisper in the ear of each player the name
of some farm animal which he must imitate
in as loud a voice as possible when the signal
is given. All of the players must cackle, crow,
whinny, moo, baa-baa, oink-oink, growl,
bark, gobble-gobble, or make some other
animal noise at the same time. This would,
of course, make a wonderfully uproarious
barnyard chorus. However, as leader, you have
secretly instructed all but one of the players
to remain silent when the signal is given.

So that when it is given, everyone is silent except for the one who has been "tricked" into cackling, barking, or baa-baaing as loudly as he can. And, of course, he feels like an idiot, and everyone laughs at him for being taken in.

You can vary the game by telling all the players except two to remain silent, and these two could be a hen and a rooster screaming at each other—cock-a-doodle-do! and cut-cut-ca-da-cut!—while everyone else rolls on the ground. Or a dog and a cat growling, barking, snarling, and hissing at each other.

Or you could vary it still further: the first time around tell everyone to make the animal sound you have given them. Everyone. Then you would have that uproarious chorus. Then the second time say that you are going to change the animals, and then whisper to all except one to be silent. He will unsuspectingly be trapped into cackling or woof-woofing or whatever you have told him or her to do.

GUESSING GAME

This can keep you busy for a long time. There are nine letters here, and a tenth one is needed to complete the series. What is the next letter? OTTFFSSEN_____The answer is "T" for ten.

O T T F F S S E N T
one two three four five six seven eight nine ten

🐌 Virginia Towsey, Washington, D.C.

ANIMAL, VEGETABLE, MINERAL

If you don't know this, your mother or camp counselor will. It's as old as the hills. It's a guessing game. One person thinks of an object, any object at all. The others, in turn, have to ask questions (with only "yes" or "no" answers) to try to guess the object.

The reason it is called Animal, Vegetable, Mineral is because the first questions try to determine the category of the object. For example, you've chosen "SALT."

First person: Is it animal?
Answer: No.
Second: Is it vegetable?
Answer: No.
Third: Is it mineral?
Answer: Yes.
Fourth: Is it a very valuable mineral?
Answer: Yes.
Fifth: Is it very rare?
Answer: No.
First: It's valuable, but it's not rare. Let's see. Is it copper?
Answer: No.
Second: Is it mined?
Answer: Yes.
Third: Is it used in industry, in the making of automobiles, for example?
Answer: No.
Fourth: Is it coal?
Answer: No.

Fifth:	Does everyone in the United States know what it is?
Answer:	Yes.
First:	Does everyone in the world know what it is?
Answer:	Yes.
Second:	Is it found in houses and homes?
Answer:	Yes.
Third:	In the bathrooms?
Answer:	Yes. Not always.
Fourth:	Is it found in kitchens?
Answer:	Yes.
Fifth:	In all kitchens?
Answer:	I'd have to say yes.
First:	A mineral in kitchens? Tin cans?
Answer:	No.
Second:	Is it ever found outside of the kitchens? Not in bathrooms, but elsewhere?
Answer:	Yes.
Third:	In dining rooms?
Answer:	Yes.
Fourth:	Silver? Forks, knives, salt cellars?
Answer:	No.
Fifth:	Salt cellars? Salt shakers? SALT?
Answer:	Yes.

And then you start over. It can be an enormous amount of fun.

John C. Scott, Arlington, Virginia

SUGAR, SALT, AND PEPPER

This has nothing to do with Vegetables and Minerals, but is a small acrobatic game. One child lies on the floor on his back with his knees pulled back over his stomach. Another child sits on the first child's feet. The child sitting on the feet can say "sugar," "salt," or "pepper," depending upon what kind of a ride he wants to get through the air. If he says "sugar," he gets a gentle push off. If he says "salt," he gets quite a shove. And if he says "pepper," the one on the floor pulls his knees back as far as he can and catapults the sitter as far and hard as he can.

🐚 Cathy Campbell, Chevy Chase, Maryland

CAR GAMES

Some of the preceding games can certainly be played while driving long distances in a car, games such as the "Ghost" game or "I'm going on a picnic, and I'm going to take with me . . . ." But the car games here can only be played in a car while driving. They cannot be played indoors.

Bury Your Horses

"On long car trips, we would each count the number of horses we each saw. Whenever a cemetery was seen, whoever first yelled out 'Bury Your Horses' would keep his count of horses, and everyone else would have to start over again from scratch." The first one to see a horse, of course, got that horse.

✍ Ellen Faryna, Perry, New York

Cows

This is played slightly differently. There are two players, and one player takes one side of the road, and the other takes the other. Each counts cows. A cemetery on the side of one of the players turns his count back to zero, and he has to start over again. At the end of an agreed upon time, the one with the most cows wins.

✍ James Moulder, Haverford, Pennsylvania

Rabbits

When you see a station wagon, say "Rabbit." The person with the most rabbits wins the game.

🐚 Unnamed informant

The Alphabet Game

"When we were young, my brothers and sisters and I often got bored on long trips. My father started us playing a game which we called the Alphabet Game. Dad would call out each letter of the alphabet, and we had to try to be the first to name an object outside the car beginning with that letter. When 'Q' came up, we would spend an hour waiting for a 'Quaker State Motor Oil' sign!

"You can vary this a little by adding to the objects outside the car (such as *house*, *insect*, *junkyard*), the letters you see on license plates. And, of course, you have the letters on billboards and signs. If you're quick, for example, you can have 'Q,' 'R,' 'S,' and 'T' from the Quaker State Motor Oil sign alone. And then you start over after 'Z.' What's a 'Z'? It would have to come from a sign or a license plate. You don't see many zebras on the highway today."

🐚 Jean Lambert, Athens, Pennsylvania

I Spy

This is like the Alphabet Game, except that you have to be very alert because the object spied must be named before it has been passed and is out of sight. Here it is: "On long journeys our family always played I Spy. 'I spy with my little eye something beginning with . . . ,' and then the person chooses something easily seen from the car window and gives only the first letter. Everyone else must guess what the object is."

🐚 Virginia Towsey, Washington, D.C.

Air Horn

"When passing a truck, the child nearest the truck driver would stick his arm out the window and make a pulling motion. Then everyone would wait to see whether the driver would respond with a pull on his air horn." Not a game, but fun.

🐚 Peter Weidlein, Mt. Kisco, New York. Peter says that "before it was outlawed, this custom was most successful on the Pennsylvania Turnpike." I wonder why it was outlawed?

Tinker-Tinker

"When we are on a car trip and the children see a Dairy Queen (ice cream, milk shakes), we all yell 'Tinker-tinker-tinker,' imitating the car's turn signal, to tell Dad we want him to turn in there."

🐚 Cynthia Barnett, Decatur, Illinois

TRICKIES

Spell STEP 10 times.
Say STEP 10 times.
Then ask: What do you do at a green light?
GO! (But many people will say STOP)

    🖎 Linda Lukow, Jericho, New York

Spell TOAST 3 times.
Say TOAST 3 times.
Spell BOAST 3 times.
Say BOAST 3 times.
What goes in the toaster?
  Bread.
(Usually people will say toast.)

    🖎 Courtney Hoover, Chevy Chase, Maryland,
collected by Sandy Bell

Say op, op, op, op ten times, quickly.
Say pop, pop, pop, pop ten times, quickly.
Say top, top, top, top ten times, quickly.
Then ask very quickly:
  What do you do at a green light?

    🖎 John Coursen, Princeton, New Jersey

Ask someone to say ten (10) ten times very
quickly.
Then ask him to spell ten (t-e-n) ten times
very quickly.
Then ask him: What is an aluminum can
made out of?
  He is likely to answer "tin" which is, of
course, wrong.

    🖎 Joey Jupiter, New York City

PUNCHING

When you see a Diamond Taxi, you can hit the person you are with, shouting at the same time: "Diamond Taxi!" (It has to be a Diamond cab, though. Others don't count.)

🦋 Kate Hayes, Washington, D.C.

When you see a man with a beard, shout "Fox-in-the-bush," and punch the person you're with in the arm. He must scream "Free!" so that you will stop punching him.

🦋 Charles Friedley, Sussex, New Jersey

On the first day of the month, you can holler, "A pinch and a punch for the first of the month!" You can then pinch and punch (once) the person with you, but he can't pinch or punch you back because you said it first.

🦋 Virginia Towsey, Washington, D.C.

JUMP ROPE

IOO

JUMP ROPE

Mother, mother, I am ill,
Call the doctor over the hill.
   In came the doctor,
   In came the nurse,
   In came the lady with the alligator
   purse.
"Measles," said the doctor.
"Mumps," said the nurse.
   "Nothing," said the lady with the
   alligator purse.

> Vernetta Raynor, Peabody Elementary
> School, Washington, D.C.

Mother, mother, I am ill,
Send for the doctor over the hill.
Doctor, doctor, will I die?
Yes, you must and so must I.
How many years will I live?
   1, 2, 3, 4 . . . . .

> Loretta Dash, Peabody Elementary School,
> Washington, D.C.

All in together!
How do you like the weather, girls?
See the teacher tapping on the window?
   Shella, shella, shoo.
   January, February, March, April,
   May, June, July, August, September,
   October, November, December.
(Each girl *runs out* on the month of her birthday.)

     Dorothy White, Peabody Elementary
    School, Washington, D.C.

In, spin,
Let Judy come in.
Out, spout,
Let Judy go out.

     Vernetta Raynor, Peabody Elementary
    School, Washington, D.C.

Suzy cute,
Suzy sweet
Can jump a hundred
On one feet!

Jaybird, Jaybird
Sitting on a rail,
Picking his teeth
With the end of his tail.
Mulberry leaves
And calico sleeves,
All school teachers
Are hard to please.

     Cleothia Hubbard, Peabody Elementary
    School, Washington, D.C.

102

Apple on a stick
Makes me sick,
Makes my heart go 2–4–6.
Not because it's dirty,
Not because it's clean,
Not because you kissed a girl
Behind the magazine.
So come on, girl,
Let's have some fun.
You can wiggle,
You can waggle,
You can do the twist,
But I betcha five dollars
You can't do this:
Close your eyes and count to ten,
If you miss, you're a big fat hen.

Pamela Lewis, who heard it chanted by "children in the neighborhood," Oxon Hill, Maryland

Milk, milk, lemonade,
Turn the corner,
Fudge is made!

🐦 Collected by Susan Niemiera, Perth Amboy,
New Jersey, from Susan Botoff, Wyndwood,
Pennsylvania

My father is a butcher,
My mother cuts the meat,
And I'm a little meatball
That runs up and down the street!

🐦 Meryl Markowitz, Oceanside, New York

Blondie and Dagwood went downtown,
Blondie bought an evening gown,
Dagwood bought a pair of shoes,
And Cookie bought the *Evening News*,
And this is what it said:
"Hop on one foot,
One foot one,
Hop on two feet,
Two feet, two feet,
Turn around, 'round, 'round,
Touch the ground, ground,
Jump out!"

Jelly in the bowl,
Jelly in the bowl,
Wiggy, waggy, wiggy, waggy,
Jelly in the bowl.

Jump one,
Jump two,
Now say Ala-ma-kanga-roo.
Jump three,
Jump four,
Now say Ding-danga-dor.
Jump five,
Jump six,
Now say just for kicks,
Luci-duci-ala-ma-scusi.
Jump seven,
Jump eight,
Now say at the fastest rate,
Christopher Morn blew his horn,
Then rode away on a unicorn.
Jump nine,
Jump ten,
Now say everything over again.

Sally Rand
Lost her fan,
Run, run, run,
As fast as you can.

All from Mary Balicki, Chicopee, Massachusetts

SCHOOL

This is a jump rope game in which the players graduate from one class to another. If you flunk in any class, you are out and do not play any more. The first one to reach college wins.

It begins:
Kindergarten: Each player runs through the rope
1st grade: Each player jumps once
2nd grade: Each player jumps twice
and so on through the 8th grade and Junior High and High School until you are a winning freshman in college.

"My favorite one of all is the one I got when I asked a five-year-old if she knew any jump rope songs. She looked at me proudly and said, 'Yes':

> Jump rope,
> Jump rope,
> Watch the girls
> Jump over the rope!"

Both from Carol Greenbaum, Jericho, New York

teases
and
horrible things
to say

108

TEASES AND HORRIBLE THINGS TO SAY TO YOUR VERY CLOSE FRIENDS AND TO OTHER PEOPLE AS WELL

Car, car,
C-A-R!
Stick your head
In a jelly jar!

Car, car,
C-A-R,
Stick your head
In a pickle jar!

✍ Doris Labie, who learned them in New York City as a child. These were yelled out by children in New York streets when an automobile came along and interrupted their game.

Yah! Yah! Sani-Flush!
Jennie brushes her teeth
With a toilet brush!

Look, look,
You dirty crook,
You stole your mother's
Pocketbook!

Susie, Susie, sauerkraut,
Does your mother know you're out?

Ink, pink, penny wink,
Oh, how you do stink!

That could be a counting-out rhyme also,
and the person on whom "stink" falls is out.

Baby, baby, suck your thumb,
Wash your face in bubble gum.
If you don't know what I mean,
Wash your face in gasoline.

Peggy Luthringer, who says that four-year-
old children at Sidwell Friends School in Washington, D.C. shout this taunt.

110

Kindergarten baby,
Stick your head in gravy,
Wrap it up in bubblegum
And send it to the Navy.

And:
"When I was in kindergarten, the First
Graders said to us:

Kindergarten baby,
Stick your head in gravy,
Wash it off with lemonade,
Then you'll be in First Grade."

🍃 Lee Sleininger, Florham Park, New Jersey

Roses are red,
Violets are blue,
Sidewalks are cracked,
And so are you.

🍃 Sophie Brawner, Chevy Chase, Maryland

Roses are red,
Violets are blue,
God gave me brains—
What happened to you?

🍃 Sandy Bell, Washington, D.C.

III

"Little children can often be very mean and do a lot of teasing. In order to get back at someone for something, we would tell a friend to look at something that wasn't there, and then we'd scream:

Made you look,
You dirty crook,
Stole your mother's pocketbook!"

> Debbie Rice, and learned in Paterson, New Jersey, 1959. A fine oldie.

When someone is staring at you:
   "Why don't you take a picture? It lasts longer!"

> Maureen Mintz, from her sister in New York

Shame, shame,
We all know your name!

> Stuart Biller, and learned at Great Neck, New York

See my finger,
See my thumb,
See my fist—
You better run!

> Debra Skopczynski, who remembered it from the 1960s in Dearborn, Michigan

112

God made the ocean,
God made the lake,
God made you
And what a mistake!

> 🖋 Brenda Lebowitz, from her grade school autograph book, New Rochelle, New York

Tattletale, tattletale,
Stick your head in the garbage pail!

> 🖋 Sharon Nash, Washington, D.C.

and:

Tattletale, tattletale,
Stick your head in the garbage pail,
Wash it off with ginger ale.
I hate you!

> 🖋 Lois Murrays, New Haven, Connecticut

A warning to tattlers:
  You snitched on Mary,
  You snitched on Sue,
  Now I'm gonna snitch on you!

> 🖋 Glen Feinberg, Yonkers, New York

Fool me once,
Shame on you!
Fool me twice,
Shame on me!

> 🖋 Arlene Eisenberg, Flushing, New York

You're a turkey!
Gobble! Gobble! Gobble!

> 🖋 Phil Paccione, Croton-on-Hudson, New York

At the end of a bad day, a teacher was asked a question by a smart-alecky kid:

"Miss Price, what are cherry pies made from?"
"Cherries."
"Well then, I was wondering—what are Eskimo pies made from?"

She probably went home and cried. Be nice to your teacher!

🌿 Greg Pennell, West Chester, Pennsylvania who was given it by the teacher, Arlene Price, Washington, D.C.

Said to a kid with a funny looking shirt: "Hey, I used to have a shirt like that before my father got a job."

🌿 Bruce Chase, Hackensack, New Jersey

A teasing reply to someone who is always saying "Hey!"

Straw is cheaper,
Grass is free,
Marry a farmer,
And you'll have all three.

🌿 Cynthia Barnett, Decatur, Illinois

And another reply, with a slight variation:

Sticks and stones may break my bones,
But names will never harm me.
Call me this and call me that,
And call yourself a big fat rat!

🌿 Rhonda Lustig, Yonkers, New York

And another goody. If someone calls you a "drip," your reply is:

A drip is a drop,
A drop is water,
Water is nature,
And nature is beautiful.
Thanks for the compliment.

🌿 Mary Balicki, Chicopee, Massachusetts

RANK OUTS AND OTHER HAPPY INSULTS

Mark Seides of Long Beach, New York, says that when he and his friends were between the ages of ten and fourteen they used to rank each other out and otherwise insult each other at lunchtime at school. "Ranking out was rarely accompanied by malicious feelings. It was as natural and common to us as our daily lunch. Lunch without ranking each other out would have been incredibly dull." But pick your lunchmates!

"Low" Rank Outs

I can rank you so low you can play jump-rope on my shoelaces.

I can rank you so low you can drown in a raindrop.

I can rank you so low you can sleep in a matchbox.

I can rank you so low you can pole vault with a toothpick.

I can rank you so low you'll need a stepladder to reach bottom.

I can rank you so low you'll need a ladder to climb out of the sidewalk cracks.

I can rank you so low you'll make Tom Thumb look like the Jolly Green Giant.

Insults

There's a lot of imagination in some of the "low" rank outs. You won't have any trouble making up a lot of your own to rank out a friend. Now come the straightaway insults which follow the rank outs:

Your face looks like a raised map.

Your teeth are like pearls. They need stringing.

I've got three minutes to spare. Tell me everything you know.

Your face looks like the pizza I ate last night.

You have a very striking face. How many times were you struck?

How much do you charge to haunt a house?

You look as though you'd dressed in a wind tunnel.

If your body were a building, it would be condemned.

You grow on me—like a wart.

Is that your nose, or are you eating a banana?

Sorry about the accident.
  What accident?
You mean you were born that way?

Did you get the car's license-plate number?
  What car?
The one that ran over your head.

That's funny. You're wearing a right shoe and a left shoe.
  What's so funny about that?
Mary told me you had two left feet.

I dreamt about you last night. Worst nightmare I've had in weeks.

Go out and play in the traffic.

Why don't you go play in quicksand?

Don't sit down too hard. You might give yourself a concussion.

Brains aren't everything. In your case, they're nothing.

Are you a man or a mouse? Squeak up!

Have fun with them, but don't take them too seriously. Remember your sense of humor.

Here are an added couple:

You look like a million dollars—green and wrinkled.

You're as romantic as a soup sandwich.

🥬 John Scott, Arlington, Virginia

And some more:

That's a nice outfit you're wearing. What style is it—early Salvation Army?

You look like you fell off a cliff and lived to tell about it!

You look as though you'd been kissed by a freight train.

Your face looks like the inside of Howe Caverns.

Your face is enough to make a rock bleed!

> Laurie Drescher, New Rochelle, New York

You're so dumb you can't walk and chew gum at the same time!

> Mike August, Silver Spring, Maryland

"My heart bleeds for you."

"Swallow a band-aid!"

> Brian Zorn, the Bronx, New York

Why be disagreeable?
With a little more effort
You can be a real stinker.

> Leslie Peak, Philadelphia, Pennsylvania

Friends like you don't grow on trees—
They swing from them!

> Carolyn Peace, Melville, New York

Go jam your toe in a pickle jar!

> Linda Coleman, Boston, Massachusetts

SCRAM!

Some not too very polite ways of telling a friend (or foe) to be on his/her way. Use them very carefully or you may wind up with a piece of beefsteak soothing a sore eye.

Put an egg in your shoe and beat it!

Make like a drop and splatter!

Make like dandruff and flake off!

Make like a tree and leave!

Make like the wind and blow!

Make like a bee and buzz off!

Make like a snake and slither away!

Make like scissors and cut out!

Mark Seides, Long Beach, New York

Kissing Games and Love and Kisses

KISSING GAMES

If you're too old for some of these games, they will remind you of the time when you weren't. And if you're not too old, they'll give you some ideas! Most of them were collected by Michele Savitzky, Glen Rock, New Jersey, from fellow students at American University in 1971. They had played them in school and highschool. The names of the students follow the description of the games.

Pick-A-Shoe

Each person tosses one of his or her shoes into a circle in the middle of the room. Someone who has been chosen to be in charge shouts, "GO," and each person must then run and pick up someone else's shoe. Then each person must kiss the owner of the shoe he or she is holding. The game is, of course, repeated.

🖎 Myrna Kaufman, Hollywood, Florida

Hide and Seek

All the players hide in the house. A finder or "IT" has been selected to look for the other players. If a boy finds another boy, they must switch places. If a boy finds a girl, he may kiss her as many times as there are people playing the game.

Jim Sessler, Amherst, New Hampshire

Two Minutes In Heaven

A girl is placed in a closet blind-folded. The boys draw lots to choose who may go in the closet with the girl for two minutes. After he comes out, the girl must guess which boy it was. The game is repeated with a different girl.

Michele Plotkin, New York City

Spin the Bottle

An empty coke bottle (or any other type) is placed in the center of a circle which the participants form, seated boy-girl-boy-girl, and so on. Someone is chosen to start the game by spinning the bottle on the floor slowly or very fast, just as he or she chooses. When the bottle stops spinning, he or she must kiss whomever it points to. Then the person who has been kissed changes places and must do the spinning. Of course, if the bottle points to someone of the same sex as the spinner, he or she must respin.

Michele Savitsky and many other students. It is one of the oldest and best known games.

Champagne

The lights are turned out and couples are dancing. A "caller" names one of three drinks. If he says "beer," the partners must hug. If he says "wine," a little kiss must follow. And if he calls "champagne," the couples may "carry on as they see fit!" After each call, partners are exchanged.

🌿 Vicki Alberg, Teaneck, New Jersey

Or instead of CHAMPAGNE, try VANILLA, CHOCOLATE, STRAWBERRY: While couples are dancing, one flavor is called. Vanilla means that you may sit on your partner's knee; chocolate means change partners; and strawberry means kiss your partner.

🌿 Michele Plotkin, New York City

Love at First Sight

Each person holds a bag over his or her head. A hole has been cut in the bag so that the mouth is exposed. When the lights go off, each person finds a kissing partner! And when the lights go back on, the bags are removed, and the kissing partner is now a dancing partner for the next dance.

🌿 Meryl Meyers, Great Neck, Long Island

Choo Choo

This is fun. The game is usually played with a large group at a party where there is access to two separate rooms. All those who already know the game line up boy-girl-boy-girl to form a train. All those not knowing the game stay in one room while the train goes "choo-chooing" into the other room. The train comes back out a minute or so later, and the last person in the train picks up a boy or girl from those not knowing the game. The train then "choo choos" back into the other room, and the door is shut. While in the closed room, the first person in the train kisses the second (not just a peck), who kisses the third, and so down the line. The last person soon assumes that he or she will be kissed in turn, but instead he or she is slapped by the next to last person. Once that person has been slapped, he or she then becomes part of the train, and they play the trick on the next unsuspecting person. The game continues until everyone has been kissed. "The expressions on the people's faces as they are slapped are fantastic."

🦚 Susan Sloane, Belmont, Massachusetts

Slap, Hug, and Kiss

Fold several pieces of paper with the words *slap, hug,* or *kiss* on the different pieces and place them in a hat. All the players then stand in a circle, and the player who is chosen (by the spin of a bottle) picks a piece of paper out of the hat which will read either "slap," "hug," or "kiss." This player then chooses his victim and either slaps, hugs, or kisses him or her, according to the instruction on the paper.

   ✍ Marilyn Swesnik, Chevy Chase, Maryland

Musical Chairs

The chairs are lined up in two rows, back to back. All the boys sit on these chairs. Music is played or a record put on, and when it is stopped, the girls who have been circling the chairs have to run and sit on the nearest boy's lap and kiss him as the lights are turned off. In a minute or two the music starts again, the lights are turned on, and the game is repeated.

   ✍ Hope Miller, East Meadow, New York

Sink or Swim

The girls sit in a row or in a half circle on chairs, and the boys line up and walk past the girls. If a girl says "Sink!" as the boy walks by, he kisses her. If she says "Swim!," he goes on to the next girl. (Be kind to the boy: say "Sink!" every so often.)

   ✍ Janice Katz, Irvington, New Jersey

Post Office

One player is given the role of mailman, and he passes out letters in pairs of As and Bs and Cs to the others playing the game. Those who have matching letters go into another room to kiss.

🌸 Bill LaFleur, Fairhaven, New Jersey

Padiddles and Padunkles

When driving, if you meet a car with one headlight out, you say "Padiddle" and kiss the person you are with. If you pass or see a car with one back light out, you say "Padunkle," and the person you are with kisses you.

🌸 Melinda McFarlin, Fort Lauderdale, Florida, remembered from her high-school days in Falls Church, Virginia

Hide and Go Seek

The first person found is kissed.

🌸 Hope Miller, East Meadow, New York

Lazy Mary

This play-party game which ends in love and kisses is well over two hundred years old, but the amazing thing is that it survived by word of mouth over the years and came to Jamie Rothstein of Woodmere, New York, from his grandmother. Play it with a group of youngsters at summer camp. The music practically sings itself, and you can make an easy tune. The conversation is between a mother and her "lazy Mary" daughter.

Mother: Lazy Mary, will you get up,
             Will you, will you, will you get up,
             Lazy Mary, will you get up,
             Will you get up this morning?

Mary: What will you give me if I get up,
             If I get up, if I get up,
             What will you give me if I get up,
             If I get up this morning?

Mother: A glass of milk and a slice of
bread,
A slice of bread, a slice of bread,
A glass of milk and a slice of
bread,
If you get up this morning.

Mary: No, mother, I won't get up,
I won't get up, I won't get up,
No, mother, I won't get up,
I won't get up this morning.

Mother: Lazy Mary, will you get up,
Will you, will you, will you get
up,
Lazy Mary, will you get up,
Will you get up this morning?

Mary: What will you give me if I get
up,
If I get up, if I get up,
What will you give me if I get
up,
If I get up this morning?

130

Mother: A bowl of soup and a slice of
cake,
A slice of cake, a slice of cake,
A bowl of soup and a slice of
cake,
If you get up this morning.

Mary: No, mother, I won't get up,
I won't get up, I won't get up,
No, mother, I won't get up,
I won't get up this morning.

Mother: Lazy Mary, will you get up,
Will you, will you, will you get
up,
Lazy Mary, will you get up,
Will you get up this morning?

Mary: What will you give me if I get
up,
If I get up, if I get up,
What will you give me if I get
up,
If I get up this morning?

Mother: A nice young man with rosy
cheeks,
With rosy cheeks, with rosy
cheeks,
A nice young man with rosy
cheeks,
If you get up this morning.

Mary: Yes, mother, I will get up,
I will get up, I will get up,
Yes, mother, I will get up,
I will get up this morning!

A nice young man is given to Lazy Mary,
and they kiss.

LOVE AND KISSES

If all the boys were to go to sea,
What a good swimmer you would be!

> 🌺 Diane Malbauer, Fairlawn, New Jersey,
> from her 1965 sixth grade autograph album

I hate to do the dishes,
I hate to do the floor,
But I love to kiss my boyfriend
Behind the kitchen door, door, door.

> 🌺 Maureen Mintz, Roslyn, New York, who
> calls it a "pattycake song" that she knew as
> a youngster in Bayside, New York

"We wore quarters in our loafers to signify
that we were 'going steady.' "

> 🌺 Peggy Luthringer, Washington, D.C., and
> now teaching at the Sidwell Friends School
> there. "This was a custom of ninth and tenth
> graders."

"If you are going steady with a boy, take
out the laces in your gym sneakers or shoes
and put them back in upside down, so that
the bow is closest to your toe."

> 🌺 Amy Singer, from friends in Junior High,
> Barrington, Rhode Island, and also from Sharon
> Weber, Brooklyn, New York

Sugar is sweet,
Lemon is sour,
How many boys
Can you kiss in an hour?

> Lindsay Dane, Franklin Square, New York,
> who learned it in the sixth grade

"My sister who is eight years old told me
how she gets a boy to like her. She makes a
ring out of a pipe cleaner and tries to get
the boys she likes to wear it."

> Kerry Klein, Plainview, New York. Nice
> trick!

Kisses are nouns, both common and proper,
Often disliked by Mamma and Papa.
Kisses spread germs, as doctors have stated,
So go kiss (Billy), he's been vaccinated!

> Meryl Markowitz, Oceanside, New York

Oh! Please don't park the car.
Oh! Please don't park the . . .
Oh! Please don't park.
Oh! Please don't.
Oh!

       🌸 Jo Anne Kessler, Brooklyn, New York, from
       a 1969 autograph album

You walked up the banister,
You closed the stairs,
You put out your bed,
You climbed into the light—
All because you kissed
Your boyfriend goodnight!

       🌸 Cindy Gross, Passaic, New Jersey

The higher up the cherry tree
The riper grows the berry,
The sooner a young man courts a girl,
The sooner they will marry.

       🌸 Traditional Tennessee and Kentucky

Love is like an insect,
Shaped like a lizard,
Crawls around the heart
And tickles the gizzard.

> Susan Cohen, Philadelphia, Pennsylvania

Keep your eye on people in love,
Because they are all blind!

> Susan Niemiera, Perth Amboy, New Jersey,
> collected from a Mrs. Batoff of Stuttgart, Germany

Your first love is always your first love.

> Barbara Zeller, Hillsdale, New Jersey, and
> given this truism by Mrs. James Greig, Hartsdale, New York

I love you much, I love you mighty,
I wish your pajamas were next to my nightie.
But don't get shocked and don't get red,
'Cause I mean on the clothesline
And not in bed!

> Susan Cohen, Philadelphia, Pennsylvania

Roses are red,
Violets are blue,
Nobody I know
Is as sweet as you!

Sailors like boats,
Babies like toys,
But all Debra likes
Are boys, boys, boys!

> 🌿 Both from Kristin Smith, Garden City, Long Island, whose sister happens to be named Debra

And a very true statement when you are in love and a young man is walking you home:

"The longest way around
Is the sweetest way home."

> 🌿 Julie Campbell, Chevy Chase, Maryland

And a teaser. When somebody asks you for a tissue, you reply:

"Tissue? I don't even know you."

> 🌿 Dora Miller, Fair Lawn, New Jersey

If your shoelace becomes untied, then it means someone is thinking of you.

> 🌿 Larry Waldman, Cincinnati, Ohio

Don't go to London,
Don't go to France,
Stay in Kansas
And give the boys a chance.

> 🌿 Debra Smith, Garden City, New York

Ashes to ashes,
Dust to dust,
If it wasn't for (Phillip),
Your lips would rust.

🌢 Jean Lambert, Athens, Pennsylvania

In order to catch a husband soon, a girl should feed the family cat from her shoe.

Never kiss a girl for the first time if it is raining.

If you think too much about a girl,
You will get a headache.

🌢 Kerry Klein, Plainview, New York. (That poses a lot of problems. What do you do about it? Hope that he has a terrible headache? Or give him a small kiss to cure it and "make it all better?")

I love you a bushel and a peck,
A bushel and a peck,
And a hug around the neck.

> ✍ Joan Alboum, East Orange, New Jersey

If you wear red and yeller,
You'll catch a feller.

> ✍ Pam Craig, Mt. Lakes, New Jersey

He kissed her by the garden gate,
Her mother heard the smack.
She didn't think it very nice,
And made her give it back.

> ✍ Kristin Smith, Garden City, New York,
> from her mother's autograph book, Denver,
> Colorado, 1942

DIVINATIONS OF LOVE:
WHO IS HE? DOES HE LOVE ME?

To discover the man you will marry, count one hundred red convertibles, look for a red-haired woman wearing a purple dress and a man with a green tie, and then wait for a boy to speak to you. The first one who does will become your husband.

> ✍ Andrea Brown, Washington, D.C. (My
> guess is that there's going to be a long, long
> wait there. It's that "red-haired woman wearing
> a purple dress" that's going to slow things
> down.)

Where Is My Man?

On New Year's Eve, a girl should go to the top of a nearby hill and yell:

"Where, where is my man?"

From whatever direction the echo of her question returns, that will be the direction from which her future husband will come.

    🌿 Elizabeth Miller, Pittsburgh, Pennsylvania, who had this from her mother

Chewing Gum Wrappers

There are two letters on the edge of the tinfoil wrapper on a stick of gum. These are the initials of the boy or girl you are to marry.

    🌿 Brenda Lebowitz, New Rochelle, New York

If you peel the tinfoil off the inside of a gum wrapper without ripping it, you will marry somebody who is very rich.

    🌿 Katherine McManus, Binghamton, New York

A Red Bird in a Tree

When you see a red bird in a tree, start slowly saying your ABCs. The letter you are saying when he flies away is the initial of your true love.

> 🦋 Judith Warrington, Seaford, Delaware, learned from her aunt in Tennessee

Apple Stems

Twist the stem of an apple while reciting the alphabet in A–B–C–D order. For each full rotation of the apple, say a letter. When the stem breaks or comes out of the apple, you will have the initial of the first name of the person you will marry.

> 🦋 This comes from all over the place and is evidently quite common: From Frannie Markunas, Dauphin, Pennsylvania; Marcia Buchwalter, Fairfax Station, Virginia; Marie Kisner, San Antonio, Texas; Amy Millman, Mount Vernon, New York, simply for starters.

To find the initial of the last name of the person, take the stem and try punching the apple, again reciting the letters of the alphabet. When the stem punches through the skin of the apple, the letter you are saying will be the first letter of his last name.

140

Buttercups

As a little girl I remember taking a buttercup and holding it under my chin. If I could see the yellow reflection, I liked butter. But if someone else does it for you and there is a yellow reflection, it means that you are in love.

🌺 Marianne Hollister, Wheaton, Maryland

Love, Hate, Friendship, Marriage

If you have a boyfriend or "lover" and would like to know how the relationship between you will turn out, simply print his name and then print yours underneath it. Then cross out all common letters and with the remaining letters recite "love, hate, friendship, marriage," and you will have your answer:

and you have: JOHNNY JONES
SUSIE SMITH

Love hate fr. mar. Love hate fr. mar.
J O N N Y J O N

Love hate fr. mar. Love
U I M I T

The last letter is Love. You will love Johnny Jones.

🌺 Patti Cohen, Dover, Delaware

Warnings

If you sing at the table while you're eating, you'll marry a crazy husband.

> 🌹 Vicki Harrowe, Bronx, New York, from a friend's grandmother

If you knit something (a sweater, mittens, scarf) for a boy you are dating, it will bring bad luck and result in the end of your relationship.

> 🌹 Ronnie Aronchick, Bradley Beach, New Jersey, from a friend in Hartsdale, New York

If you have a bad temper when you are young, you will never marry.

> 🌹 Helen Metaxas, Margate, New Jersey, and Karen Coburn, Queens, New York

ah youth!

SMALL BOYS

What are five things
small boys are never
without?
  a pea shooter
  a water pistol
  baseball cards
  a hole in their pants
  a runny nose

🖋 Lonnie Bunch, Belleville, New Jersey

"A five-year-old boy in my group at camp
bit a girl. When I asked him why he did it,
his reply was: 'I'm a German shepherd, and
they bite.' "

🖋 Judy Richman, Maywood, New Jersey

"When I was little, there used to be a neighborhood call by which you found out which
of your friends were home from school. The
person would scream out, 'Do-uh-ah!,' and
if there was an answering 'Cha-cha-cha!,'
then you knew you had someone to play with.
This call still exists among the little kids in
the neighborhood."

🖋 Ann Sherman, Hampton, Virginia

"In order to exclude further participants in our games, we would shout, 'Golden gates are closed.' "

🦋 Mark Seides, Long Beach, New York

HOW OLD ARE YOU? 7-8-12-14?

These are all from Rob Stirling and Danny Jackson of Oswego, New York, and my guess is that they were about seven. Rob Stirling graduated from American University in 1974, and these reports are his:

"It was customary to wear a baseball cap to monster movies so that you could hide your face behind the cap when you were scared, but still see out the little holes in the top of the cap.

"In the Fall all the kids in my neighborhood would collect horse chestnuts and string them together to make jewelry for our mothers. The leftover chestnuts were saved to put inside snowballs.

"At Christmas, the older kids would put the really little kids (preschool to first grade) who still believed in Santa Claus on sleds and take them about three blocks from our street (where they weren't allowed to go alone), tell them we were at the North Pole, and give them a tour. 'That house is where dolls are made. The reindeer are in the backyard there . . . .'

"Danny Jackson and I were the only kids our age in the neighborhood, so each year we held an Easter Basket Hunt for the smaller kids. We would make up two baskets of candy and hide them in different places. We would then hide two separate sets of clues around the yard, each clue telling where the next clue (and eventually the basket) would be found. We then divided the little kids into two teams (the Bunnies and the Snakes) and sent them off after the baskets. The team that found their basket first won an extra ration of candy in their basket. When the Snakes won, they would sing, 'When a Snake meets a Bunny comin' through the rye, then the Snake will eat the Bunny, and the Bunny will cry.' The Bunnies didn't have a song.

"On rainy days we would all put on our army helmets and get our toy guns and play 'D-Day,' which consisted of running a few feet in the park, diving into the mud, firing a few rounds, getting up, running a few more feet, and so on. We would all be on the same side and would charge an imaginary enemy.

"After the parades on TV were over on Thanksgiving Day, all the kids in the neighborhood would go to Danny Jackson's house and crayon pictures of turkeys and pilgrims on paper napkins. We would then bring these napkins to our mothers, who would use them to decorate the dinner table.

"Each summer my friend Danny Jackson and I would hold a carnival, the profits from which went to buy malt balls, monster cards, and comic books, much to the chagrin of our parents. The rides and games we provided for the neighborhood included: pitching pennies into jars; getting pushed down a small hill in my backyard, blindfolded; ring toss; a stagecoach ride, which consisted of being pulled around my house in my wagon by Danny or me wearing a cowboy hat, being 'held up' in my side yard by whomever wasn't the driver, shooting the outlaw, and returning to the starting place (some years we put on face masks and had a Submarine Ride instead); and our house of horrors, which was the tool shed with monster pictures on the walls, a rubber spider hanging from the ceiling, and Danny with a flashlight hiding behind the lawnmower, flashing the light and talking in a spooky voice. Rides and games cost from 1 to 4¢ each. Lemonade and popcorn (courtesy of our parents) were sold as refreshments."

Rob Stirling, Oswego, New York. He writes well and easily, and I would not mind seeing a whole book on "Danny Jackson and I." Yes?

DIMPLES

"When I was 6 years old, my friend Jimmy, who had dimples, told me that when he was a baby his mother was mad at him and pinched his cheeks so hard she left dents. I was very upset with that explanation and decided to consult with my godfather who also had dimples.

"I remember well telling him how Jimmy got his dimples. But my godfather told me that he got his dimples when he was born. His mother was so happy to see him that she kissed him on each cheek. I believed him."

 🌷 Jamie Rothstein, Woodmere, New York

If you want dimples, sleep on a button.

 🌷 Judy Deutsch, Syosset, New York

A VICE-PRESIDENT

"One of my aunts was told at the age of seven that her mother had been elected vice-president of a women's club, and upon hearing the news became hysterical because she thought her mother would have to move to Washington."

 🌷 Bruce Rosenstein, Scranton, Pennsylvania

HAVE YOU BEEN NAUGHTY RECENTLY?

"In our family it's very easy to tell when you're in trouble and when you're not. When you're not, you are called by your nickname (for me, it's Susie), and when you are in trouble, it's by your full name, said *very* sternly, with emphasis placed on the middle name (Susan *Diane* Gilbert)."

☙ Susan Gilbert, Overland Park, Kansas

In a reprimanding tone:
"If I've told you once, I've told you a thousand times."

☙ Jay Bass, Bethesda, Maryland

To an unruly child:
"It's just a good thing you weren't twins."

☙ Cynthia Barnett, Decatur, Illinois

HOW TO GET MONEY

1. Ask your grandparent.
2. Flip pennies in the bathroom at school. The penny closest to the wall wins them all.
3. Look for return bottles by the supermarket or wherever. Then return them for 2¢ for a little bottle and 5¢ for a big bottle.
4. Help the paper boy deliver his papers. Usually I got 2¢ for any paper I delivered.

☙ Bruce Chase, Hackensack, New Jersey

150

WET CEMENT

"Every time wet cement was laid for sidewalks, we used either to put our initials, footprints, or handprints in the cement. After the cement hardened and in later days, the big thing was to say—when you walked past —that that was *your* sidewalk."

FLAT PENNIES

"On the way to Junior High School, we used to have to cross over the railroad tracks. What we used to do was to put pennies, nickels, and broken glass on the tracks and then wait for the train to go over them. The big thing was to walk around with a flattened coin in your pocket."

TEASING THE POLICE

"The kids used to have a lot of fun running away from cops. Many times we used to set off firecrackers in the park, then call the police to complain on ourselves, so that the police would come. More often than not they would come with flashing lights, surround us, and send us home."

All three from Bruce Chase. The last one you must consider as history and not to be practiced at all, at all. The police have much more to do than to chase youngsters pulling pranks. And they might not think they were pranks, either! Someone might get very badly hurt. Use judgment in what you do!

LICORICE

In THE HODGEPODGE BOOK I said that licorice was made from old rubber boots. It is not, of course, unless you want to believe so. Now, here is a licorice race. Try it with a friend at recess with the other kids watching and cheering.

Take a long, thin piece of licorice, fold it over, and make a red pencil mark in the middle at the fold point. Then you take one end in your teeth, and your friend takes the other end. Now have a race to see who can chew the faster or fill his mouth the quicker in order to get to the middle. Whoever gets to the middle first is the winner.

You'd better get rid of the licorice one way or another before you go back to class, or you'll choke on the first question the teacher asks you. And how could you recite a poem? No. Strictly for recess.

Leslie Weber, New Rochelle, New York

152

JINX ON A COKE

When you are talking with someone and you both say the same thing at the same time, one of you shouts: "Jinx on a coke!" And that same person starts counting to ten. The other person must be quick and shout: "Stop!" But the second person still owes the first as many cokes as the first person was able to count before being "Stopped."
  "Jinx on a coke! One, two, three . . ."
  "Stop!"
He owes three cokes.

> ✌ Melinda McFarlin, Fort Lauderdale, Florida, from her elementary school days in Falls Church, Virginia

And some variations on this business of saying the same thing at the same time:

NICKS

"When I was in grade school and two of us said the same thing at the same time, one would shout 'NICKS!' The one who didn't shout 'NICKS' had to suffer a punch to the shoulder by the other person. Many a day I went home with black and blue arms."

> ✌ Chris Scully, Sparrowbush, New York

A FOOLISH VISITOR

When two people say something at the same time, expect a foolish visitor.

> ✌ Jerry Malitz, Brooklyn, New York, and learned from his grandmother

SHAKESPEARE

When two people say something at the same time, you should punch the other person on the arm and shout, "Shakespeare!"

🖎 Laurie Saltz, Wayne, New Jersey

JINX

When two people say the same thing at once, they both start saying, "Jinx, 1, 2, 3, 4, 5, 6, 7, 8, 9, 10, Cheeseburger! You owe me a a coke." The first one to finish, gets the coke.

🖎 Mary Lanagan, Chevy Chase, Maryland

OUR WISH WILL NEVER BE BROKEN

If you and your friend both say the same thing at the same time, link little fingers together, push your thumbs together, and make a wish. Then:
The first person says: "What goes up the chimney?"
The second person: "Smoke."
The first person: "Your wish and mine will never be broken!"

🌺 Maggie Miles, learned from her mother-in-law in New Hampshire. (This can be much more complicated, of course, but I like this very simple way of making a wish that "will never be broken!" Easy to remember, and both persons get their wish, and nobody gets punched.)

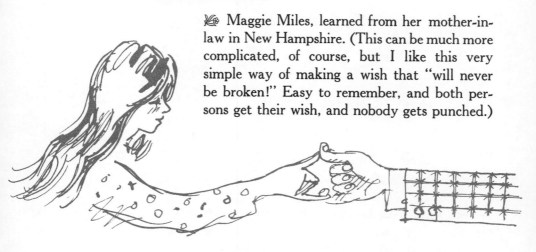

BREAD AND BUTTER

If two people are walking along and are forcibly separated by a tree or pole, for example, when they come together again, they must each say, "Bread and Butter." If it should happen a second time, they must each say, "Ham and Eggs."

🌺 Eve Wright, Garrison, New York

And one which is slightly different:

When two people are separated by a post or something like that, one person says "Bread and Butter," and the other person says "Butter and Bread." This shows that nothing can come between them.

🌿 Collected by Judith Warrington at American University from her roommate who came from the Canal Zone

TOUCH BLUE

When you and the person you are with walk around opposite sides of something (a tree, a post, a pole), you must say the following:
   "Cheese and crackers."
   "Butter and eggs."
   "What goes up the chimney?"
   "Smoke."
   "What goes down?"
   "Santa Claus."
(Link pinkies)
   "Touch blue and your wish will come true."
   "Touch glass to make it last."

🌿 Kathie Friedley, who heard it from children in Sussex, New Jersey

STORY JOKE

"I asked my seven-year-old brother to tell me his favorite joke or story, and this was his choice."

Marvin ran to his father. "Father," he yelled, "Andy just swallowed my ten cents!" So father shook Andy. He shook him, and shook him, and shook him. At last a dime came out of his mouth. "Here it is!" said Marvin's father. "Here is your dime." "But this is not my dime," cried Marvin. "Andy swallowed ten pennies!"

🖎 Margie Stegman, Norwalk, Connecticut

ZAP!

A wicked witch was walking along and she saw a little boy. She said, "Zap! You're a goon!" and the boy was one. She walked some more and cast a spell on a cat—the cat was a goon. She went further and saw a rabbit, and Zap!—Hare today and goon tomorrow.

🖎 Erica Loewenthal, New York City

ARTIFICIAL RESPIRATION

A conversation between Shawn, age 10, and Sabrina, age 8. Shawn: "I bet you don't know what artificial respiration is." Sabrina: "I do so! It's fake sweat!"

    🐝 Marilyn Swesnik, Chevy Chase, Maryland

NICKNAMES FOR CHILDREN WITH BRACES

"Cathy Gordon, an eleven-year-old in Gaithersburg, Maryland, wears braces on her teeth, and I asked her what some of the nicknames are that she is called:
   metal mouth
   tinsel teeth
   fence face
   shiny smile
"When is the train coming through?"

    🐝 E. Neil Norris, Washington, D.C.

One more from Richard Harris:
   tin grin

And two from Phillip Paccione:
   Hi-Ho, Silver!
   foil face

KOOTIES (OR COOTIES)

Kooties: When children want to tease another child at recess for some reason or another, they say that the child has the "kooties." They use the term as though it were a contagious disease.

Kooty Shot: If you are touched by a person who is said to have the kooties, you get the kooties, too, and you have to get a kooty shot. The shot consists of being touched on the shoulder with an ice cream stick. This will cure.

Kooty Base: If the person with the kooties comes toward you, run to the bicycle rack. This is considered a place where you can be safe from a kooty carrier.

🖎 Meryl Markowitz, Oceanside, New York

PINK BELLY

"My little brother Peter and I used to gang up against my older brother, Christopher, hold him down on the ground, lift up his shirt, and slap him (not too hard) on the stomach. Individually, the slaps are not painful, but if you can keep it up for long enough, the stomach turns red. This is called a 'pink belly.'"

🖎 Megan Holbrook (from her childhood), Wantagh, New York

SNOW

Snow Angels are pretty and lots of fun, even though snow gets down your back and into your shoes.

1. Fall down backward onto a clean patch of snow.
2. Move your arms up and down to make the wings.
3. Move your legs in and out to make the dress.
4. Get up carefully without messing up the figure.

Snow Ice-Cream Sundaes: On clean, fresh, hard-packed snow, pour hot (rich) maple syrup or a mixture of brown sugar and water. It hardens on the snow and makes a delicious winter treat. (It is not really a sundae, because what you will be eating will be the "frozen" syrup. But it is wonderfully good!)

Snow Ice Cream: Stir together handfuls of snow with cream, sugar, and vanilla to make soft, delicious ice cream.

Susan Gilbert, Kansas.

If you live near a playground, make a huge pile of snow at the bottom of a slide—and then slide down onto it. Whoosh!

School children made snowballs and rolled them home to their front yards. There was a contest to see who could make the biggest snowball.

Linda Selde, Washington State
All of the above are from Janice Keidel, Arlington, Virginia, who had them at first hand or collected them from her friends like Linda Selde and Susan Gilbert

CUSTOMS

Fourth of July

At the Fourth of July Fair on Cranberry Island, Maine, quarters, dimes, and nickles are placed in a haystack. On a given signal, the children all dive into the haystack and retrieve as many coins as they can grab!

Peggy Luthringer, of Washington, D.C., who says that this July Fair game was "for children of all ages."

Mother's Day

"Between the ages of six and ten, every Mother's Day a certain group of my friends and I would sneak out of our houses at eight in the morning and pick flowers for our mothers."

Meryl Green, as done in Queens, New York, in the late 1950s and early 1960s. A very nice gesture which I'm sure the mothers appreciated.

May Day

May Day baskets are a very pleasant small town tradition. "In Montezuma, Iowa, where we lived until I was seven years old, all the kids delivered May Day baskets of flowers to their friends. If they were seen by the person they were delivering it to, they had to kiss that person which, at that age, was a most painful and almost unbearable experience— although, I admit, I let a few people catch me at their doors."

🐚 Melinda McFarlin, Fort Lauderdale, Florida

SCHOOL TIME

Examination

Now I lay me down to rest,
I pray I pass tomorrow's test;
If I should die before I wake
That's one less test I'll have to take.

🐚 Linda Lukow, Jericho, New York

Whispering in Class

If you want to whisper in class without being caught, knock on a tree on your way to school.

Chiquita Banana

I'm Chiquita banana
And I'm here to say:
"Get rid of your teacher
The easy way.
Put a banana peel
On the floor,
And watch her go flying
Out the door!"

🍌 Maureen Mintz,
Roslyn, New York

And a Variant

(You're beginning to catch on to what a
"variant" is, aren't you?)

Tra la la boom-dee-ay,
Tra la la boom-dee-ay,
Eat bananas all the day,
Throw the peels on the floor,
Watch the teacher slide out the door!
Tra la la boom-dee-ay!

🍌 Harvey Samachson, Trenton, New Jersey

But watch out for her when she comes back!

Time to Go to School

If a child is able to reach across the top of his head with his right arm and touch his left ear, he is old enough to go to school.

🌿 Joyce Robertson, Oyster Bay, New York, from her childhood. Try that out on the little kids! True or not?

Spelling

**I before E except after C,
This is a rule for you and for me.
If you learn this very well,
You will do well
When you spell.**

🌿 Alex Evers, Yonkers, New York. But have you ever noticed how weird it is that there is always an exception to every rule? How do you spell "weird"?

How to Pass a Test

If you sleep on the book (preferably under your pillow) which is the subject of your test, you will do wonderfully well on the test the next day.

🌿 There may be a little bit of truth in this belief which comes from Megan Holbrook's mother in New York. With the book there, you will be thinking of it and the subject as you go off to sleep. Also in the morning, it will be the first thing you are aware of. You may be a little better prepared. But it doesn't hurt to study a lot either.

BABYSITTERS

Actually they are not babies, but small, squirming, ingenious little devils full of all sorts of excuses. Here are reports from babysitters and "babies" who once were.

The most common excuses or pleadings:

Mommy told *me* I could stay up as late as I want!
Just five more minutes!
The other babysitter always lets me.

> 🖎 Wendy Sacks, Newton Centre, Massachusetts, who reports that she has heard them from youngsters "all over."

"There were various ways to handle babysitters.

"One was to act nice and very innocent. Then you could ask if you could stay up late and usually she would say, 'yes.'

"Another way was to tell the babysitter that you always do this particular something. This usually made her a little uneasy, and she would usually let you do whatever you had dreamed up."

> 🖎 Bruce Chase, Hackensack, New Jersey. Little kids are little demons!

BIRTHDAYS

There is a belief that everyone is born possessing all the knowledge that is in the world. Everything. But before an infant breathes its first breath, an angel taps it sharply just above its upper lip, causing the infant to forget everything. This explains the little indentation above everyone's lip.

🕮 Debra Chaykin, Brooklyn, New York

And another explanation for the same thing. Folklore is not fixed, but it changes all the time. Here is an example of the same thing and of the change also:

Babies are made in Heaven and, because they are with God there, they know all the secrets of the universe. But these are secrets that mortals are not meant to know until they are with God again. To remind babies not to tell these secrets when they are born, the last thing that God does, before he sends a baby down to earth to be born, is to place His finger lightly over its lips and say, "Sh-sh-h-h." His finger leaves a vertical impression above the lip. (True? You can look in the mirror to see yours, or pucker up your lip and feel it. It's a nice belief, isn't it?)

🕮 M. Elayne Smith, Rochester, New York

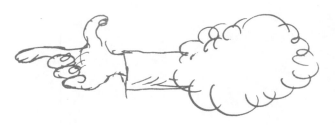

Roses are red,
Violets are blue,
Today is your day—
Happy Birthday to you!

✍ Dora Miller, Fair Lawn, New Jersey

Kings and Queens and Princes, too,
Want to wish you all that's due, so . . .
Wishday, Washday, what do you say?
Birthday—Happy Birthday to you!

✍ Collected by Maureen Mintz from Sandy
Ruben, Cherry Hill, New Jersey

"At birthday parties we used to sing this
teasing song after the traditional birthday
song:

Happy Birthday to you,
Happy Birthday to you,
You look like a monkey,
And you smell like one, too."

✍ Sandy Bell, Washington, D.C.

On your birthday you should receive a spanking—or a spank—for every year of your age,
plus one for good luck, and a pinch to grow
an inch.

If the moon is full on your eighth birthday,
you will live a long time. (You can check to
see whether it *was* full—if you're older than
eight—by looking up the date in old almanacs
or in a special book which gives all the dates
of all the years. Ask your librarian. She'll
help you. Or you can write to your newspaper
or to the publishers of almanacs.)

✍ Penny Tamsen, Newburgh, New York

If you blow out all the candles on your birthday cake with one blow, any wish that you make will come true.

Everyone knows that, but have you heard these two?

If you don't blow out all the candles on your birthday cake, you have a boyfriend for every candle left. (No cheating! Try blowing them all at once even if you want five boyfriends.)

And this:

If one candle is not blown out with all the others, that candle, still lighted, must be passed from one child to the next and to the next and next. Whoever is holding the candle when it goes out will catch the measles.

🌿 Joy Huston, Sydney, Australia

When it is your birthday, you must cut the first piece of the birthday cake while making a wish. If you cut more than one piece, the wish will not come true.

> 🌿 Virginia Towsey, Washington, D.C.

Cutting the part of your birthday cake with your name on it will bring you bad luck.

> 🌿 Stuart Biller, Great Neck, New York

Before cutting your birthday cake, you must rub out your name on the cake, because it is bad luck to cut through your name.

> 🌿 Sharon Scheinthal, New Hyde Park, New York

Don't cry on your birthday. It means bad luck for the entire following year.

> 🌿 Janice Polizzi, Northvale, New Jersey

Eat figs at your birthday breakfast for luck in your new year.

> 🌿 Suzan Marie Graham, Bloomfield, New Jersey

TELEPHONE PRANKS

"One of us would call up a grocery store and ask whomever answered, 'Do you have pigs' feet?' After checking, the clerk would return and say, 'Yes.' Then we'd reply, 'Wear socks and no one will notice.'"

    ✒ Richard Jaszczult, Alexandria, Virginia

"As a youngster I used to get together with my friends to make prank phone calls. To a tobacco store: 'Do you have Prince Albert in a can? You do? Then why don't you let him out?'

To a home owner: 'Is your refrigerator running? It is? Then you'd better hang up and catch it.'"

    ✒ Beverly Feinstein, Harworth, New Jersey

Call anyone up and say, "Hello, this is the phone company. We are working on your line at the present time. Therefore please do not answer your phone or call anyone. If you should, our man will receive a heavy electric shock and possibly be electrocuted." Then hang up, and in a minute or two call back. Let the phone ring three or four times, and then hang up again. Then call back and let the phone ring and ring. The chances are that the phone will be answered. When it is, scream!

🌿 Jeannette Paroly, West Orange, New Jersey

> Hello, is Bill there?
> No, there is no Bill here.

(*A few minutes later*)
> Hello, is Bill there?
> No!

(*again*)
> Hello, is Bill there?
> No! There isn't any Bill here!

(*and last*)
> Hello, this is Bill. Have there been any messages for me?

🌿 Susan Blumenfeld, Oceanside, New York

172

Is John Wall there?
No.

Well, is Suzy or Sharon Wall there?
No.

Are there any Walls there?
No.

Well, you better hurry up and get out before the roof caves in.

🐚 Peggy Stone, Cresskill, New Jersey

or a variant:

1st call: Hello, is Betty Wall there?
I'm sorry, you have the wrong number.

5 minutes later: Hello, is John Wall there?
No, you've got the wrong number.

5 minutes later: Hello, is Bob Wall there?
No, there are no Walls in this house.
How do you hold the ceiling up?

🐚 Glen Feinberg, Yonkers, New York, collected from Barbara Brownstein, Yonkers, New York, 1965

ANSWERING THE PHONE

There are various ways of answering the phone which can be momentarily confusing to the person calling. The best known ones are those that go something like this:

"Joe's Bakery, which crumb do you want?"

"The City Zoo, rabbit speaking."

"Pennsylvania Station ticket reservation. Where do you want to go and at what time?"

These are fairly run-of-the-mill. However, here's one that is not:

When your phone rings, answer it, but instead of saying "Hello," say "May I please speak to _____?" If done correctly and seriously, it usually creates a certain amount of confusion, because the caller may momentarily go out of his mind and think that his number is being called instead of he himself being the caller.

🖉 All from Diane Taub, Plainfield, New Jersey

Here is a rather pleasant and amusing one. When the phone rings:

"Through the grace of God, and the invention of Alexander Graham Bell, you have just been connected with the (Smith's) residence."

🖉 Melinda McFarlin, Fort Lauderdale, Florida

THE MAIL

THE MAIL

There are many things that you can write on either the front or back of an envelope of a letter you are mailing to a friend. On the front, by way of instruction to postman:

D—liver
D—letter
D—sooner
D—better
D—later
D—letter
D—madder
D—getter.

   🌿 Linda Lukow, Jericho, New York

Postman, Postman,
Don't be slow,
Be like Elvis
And go, man, go!

   🌿 Janice Keidel, Arlington, Virginia

And also on the front, you can be nice to a
friend by writing:
Gee, how I
> Miss Cathy Smith
> 1232 East 28th Street
> Brooklyn, New York

> 🌸 Also from Janice Keidel

On the back of the envelope, there are all sorts
of things:
SWAK—Sealed With A Kiss
SWALCAKWS—Sealed With A Lick 'Cause
A Kiss Won't Stick

> 🌸 Collected by Bobbi Berman from Wendy
> Maimon, at Camp Wohelo, Waynesboro, Penn-
> sylvania

LWMT—Licked With My Tongue

> 🌸 Janice Keidel again

Postman, Postman,
Do your duty,
Deliver to Jane,
The American beauty!

> Janice Katz, Irvington, New Jersey

If you think that the letter is going to go
astray:
   If found by person, deliver by mail;
   If found by male, deliver in person.

And also, if you haven't heard from someone
in a long time:
   Roses are red,
   Violets are blue,
   I'm still alive—
   How about you?

> Both from Linda or Janice or Bobbi, I'm
> not absolutely certain which

On the back of a letter (or front, for that matter) you can write the letters R. M. A., which
stand for Remember Me Always. Nobody but
your best friend will know what they mean,
and the postman will be puzzled.

    🖎 Judy Iwler, Leetsdale, Pennsylvania

And also on the back of a letter, you can say
to your friend:
Me 4 You
      e
      v
      e
      r
And top it off with an S.W.A.K. if you want.

    🖎 Erica Loewenthal, New York City

Arnold Stone of Baltimore had fun corre-
sponding with a friend in New Jersey, and
they played "pen-pal games" with each other.
For example, Arnold received a letter from his
friend, and this was it:
    "Hi, just thought I'd drop you a line."

And Arnold wrote back:
    "I've got a lot of time today, so I'll write
you a long letter. A"

If you drop a fork by accident, you will get a
letter in the next mail. Or you should get it.

    🖎 Susan Burns, Derby, Vermont

WISHES

WISHES

All of the following wishes and ways of wish-making were, with some exceptions, sent to me in letters from 8- to 11-year-old youngsters in this country and Canada. They are quite special and wonderful. Do you have your own special way of making a wish?

If a ladybug lands on you, make a wish when it is leaving, and then don't talk for three minutes, and your wish will come true.

If you see a ladybug, hop around in a circle three times, and then make the sound of the first animal that comes into your mind. Just for luck count to seven.

🖎 Ann Sydeman, Los Angeles, California

When you find an acorn, put it in your pocket. Keep it for seven days. At the end of seven days, throw it away onto some grass. Make a wish while doing so. A green acorn is best.

🖎 Dwyn Smith, Portland, Oregon

If it's your birthday, and you want to make a wish, go ahead. It's your day.

If you're good and don't tell a lie all day, make a wish. (If you tell five lies one day, you will have bad luck the next day.)

🖎 Kathy Rivers, San Jose, California

If you have a stuffed animal, kiss the right leg five times and make a wish. (first letter)

If the animal has 4 legs, it is the *back* right leg. I have a Teddy bear. Yes, it can make a difference. If it is a dog, it is the front right leg. But any other animal the back leg. (second letter) P.S. Yes, we have a dog. Its name is Susie. She has had so many puppies we are getting sick of it!

🖎 Kimberley Box, Houston, Texas

If you see a duck in a pond, make a wish and say "QUACK!" If the duck quacks back, your wish will come true. If there is more than one duck in a pond, and more than one quacks back, your wish will come true soon.

When you find a piece of featherdown floating in the air, catch it. Make a wish, and blow it away.

Catch a firefly in your hand. Start counting to ten, and if he blinks his light five times while you are counting, quickly make a wish and let him go.

If you see a cat washing, guess what part will be washed next. If you're right, make a wish and it will come true.

🌿 Priscilla Rowe, Richmond, Virginia

Did you know that if you wish on three birds on a telephone wire before they fly away, you'll get your wish?

🌿 Karen Doner, Sands Point, New York

I am twelve years old. When I was ten my sister was born, and I wanted a sister, so I wished for a brother (but I didn't want one), and I got a sister. (I have a brother.)

🌼 Jeanie Powell, Decatur, Georgia. Wishes, like dreams, can very often come in opposites. Depends upon what you believe.

When you go under a tunnel or bridge, put your hands flat on the top of your car in the inside, and close your eyes the second you go under, and don't open them 'till you get out and not before. Say your wish over and over when you are in the tunnel, and your wish will come true.

🌿 Tracy Rogers, Phoenix, Arizona

If you see a white horse, say:
  White horse, white horse,
  Good luck to me,
  Good luck to every
  White horse I see!
Spit over your shoulder and think of a wish. It will come true.

🌿 Collected by Sandra Fellner from R. Mercer ("our janitor"), George McKillop School, Lethbridge, Alberta, Canada

When you see the first robin in the Spring, look at him twice, then go up to the tree where he is and tap it. Then make a wish.

🌿 Michele McShane, Bennington, Vermont

When you visit a church for the first time, you can make three wishes. My mother heard this from her mother, my grandmother, but I don't know where she learned it.

✍ Joseph Internicola, Olmsted Falls, Ohio

When I got new shoes, I made a wish and it came true.

✍ Nina Urchenko, Hyde Park, New York

Wish on a new pair of shoes.

Shut your eyes and wish on a wishing pond.

✍ Ricky Sangar, George McKillop School, Lethbridge, Alberta, Canada

When I make a wish, I get a lucky stone and throw it up four times, catch it three times, and the fourth time I drop it. Then I tramp on it and make a wish, and then I pick it up and throw it into some bushes. Then a few days later my wish comes true.

✍ Lori Ann Jackson, Salem, Ohio

You make a big, big hopscotch, and while you are hopping on one foot you hold your breath for as long as you can. Then at the end, you make a wish.

If you find a turtle on his back, pick him up, turn him over, and then you have four wishes.

🎀 Elizabeth Casella, Phoenix, Arizona

If you find a dandy lion and make a wish and blow all the seeds off at one blow, your wish will come true.
P.S.—This wishing hint has been around very long and it is one of my favorite wishes, so I decided to tell you about it.

🎀 Renee Tempest, Phoenix, Arizona.—Thank you, Renee.

If you make a wish with a watermelon seed stuck onto your forehead, your wish will come true.

🎀 Barbara Lee, West Yarmouth, Massachusetts, and collected from her roommate at American University, Shelly Daitz, Great Neck, New York

I have a wish. First you find a four leaf clover. Then when you go to bed, put it under your pillow. Then you wake up at midnight, touch your toe and kiss the clover three times. Make a wish while you are kissing the clover. Your wish will come the next or in two days.

And also:

When there is a new moon, go outside and curtsy seven times to the new moon and make a wish. If you are a boy, you have to bow seven times to the new moon. This is a Swedish wish. My mother is Swedish, and she told me this wish.

🖎 Mona Marquardt, Bowling Green, Ohio

If you take a piece of string and tie it in seven knots around the middle finger of your right hand while making seven wishes, and the boy you like takes it off after seven days, your wishes will come true. (This was practiced by sixth graders. I believe it.)

🖎 Jackie White, Medinah North School, Illinois

Your wish will come true if you wish on green M & M's. Only green will do!!

🐛 Susie Markunas, Dauphin, Pennsylvania. On the other hand, I had a letter from a young man who said that only red would do. I guess you can pick your own colors, but you have to stick with them.

Now here are a delightful batch of wishes from Oregon. Charlene Perkins who teaches the third grade at the May Street School in Hood River, Oregon, asked her little charges to write down different ways that they had of making wishes, and then she very kindly sent them to me. I can't put them all in here, but I'm sure you'll like those that are here. Miss Perkins said of the children's "letters" or "notes": "Please be patient with their spelling and handwriting—they struggle so with both." Didn't we all at one time! And don't some of us still. So, I've "corrected" the spelling where it was needed, but I think the children have done very well. And anyhow, there is an enormous amount of imagination here. Here goes from third graders from Hood River, Oregon:

If you see a rusty can in some bushes, make a wish, pat it on the bottom five times. Stomp it. Then throw it in the garbage. Your wish will come true.

If you see a plant that has just started growing, put water on it. If it's not in the sun, put it in the sun. Then your wish will come true.

If you see a cat that is black with green eyes, make a wish. Pet it ten times. Your wish will come true.

If you see a white horse with black spots, feed it some grass. Pet him ten times. Feed him some more. Your wish will come true.

All of those from Stacey Franks, and believe you me if she doesn't turn into a wonderful woman around the house, a farmer or rancher in her own right, an ecologist, or something such, then I'm a monkey's uncle. Which reminds me of a joke: What did the monkey say when his sister gave birth to a baby? Answer: "Well, I'll be a monkey's uncle!"

If you find a dime, put it in your ear, count to five, then your wish will come true.

🌿 Billy Phillips

If you see a mermaid, swim after it, and if you can't catch it, make a wish. Remember, you can't swim there again.

🌿 Grant Stikney

Wish on the first dinosaur bone you dig up.

The first squirrel you see that has only one brown hair, make a wish, then clap your hands five times, turn around, and don't talk to anyone for half an hour.

When you scale a fish, bet how many scales will be on the floor. The winner makes a wish and says: I wish for a fish in a dish.

🐛 Laura Stager

When you see a cloud and it looks like a dog, find a frog and kiss it. When you see a beer bottle, make a wish and break it, and put the glass in the trash can, and if you don't put it in, you will have bad luck.

Every time you see red tennis shoes (ten-shose), you can make a wish.

🐛 Larry Fisk

If you find a peanut, kiss it three times, then set it back down where you found it, and your wish will come true.

🐛 Susanna Warrenka

The rest of these wishes were gathered by students of mine at American University, remembered either out of their own childhood, taught to them by their parents, or picked up by them from classmates and friends at school or camp. They are somewhat more traditional than those from Hood River, and you have probably heard and practiced many of them.

When you see a mail truck, cross your fingers and make a wish. You must then keep your fingers crossed until you see a dog. Then uncross them, and the wish will come true sooner or later.

    🌿 Roberta Waldbaum, Maywood, New Jersey

When you see a mail truck, cross your fingers. When you then see something which is the color of navy blue, then you can uncross your fingers and make a wish.

    🌿 Nancy Gendler, South Hampstead, New York

When you are driving under a bridge, place your hand on the roof of the car, toot your horn, and make a wish. If a train is going over the bridge at the same time, you may make a double wish.

    🌿 Leslie Fink, North Bellmore, New York

If you can peel the silver foil from the wax paper on a gum wrapper without tearing it, you may make a wish which will come true.

    🍃 Ellen Boorstein, Roslyn, New York

When you eat a piece of pie (or cake), cut the point and set it aside to make a wish on. After you have eaten the rest of the piece, put the point in your mouth, and make a wish. Repeat the wish to yourself as you chew it, and then repeat the wish a third time as you swallow. Your wish will come true.

    🍃 Collected by Judith Harrington from her roommate from the Canal Zone

Take a fluffy dandelion, make a wish, and blow the fluff off. The number of blows required to strip the dandelion of its fluff stands for the number of years it will take for your wish to come true.

    🍃 Nancy Van Alstine, Bethesda, Maryland

Whenever you are driving over railroad tracks always lift your feet when crossing the tracks, and make a wish. It is considered bad luck not to lift your feet (the driver excepted), and you may well lose a boyfriend by ignoring this very sound advice.

    🍃 Bobbi Berman, Baltimore, Maryland

"Wish bugs" are the dandelion seeds that float in the air. It was very special to catch one, make a wish on it, and throw it high into the air again. You hopefully watched it fly away, but if you saw it fall to the ground, your wish would not come true.

🌿 Janice Keidel, Arlington, Virginia

If the clasp on a necklace chain works its way from its proper position at the back of the neck to the front of the neck near the pendant, make a wish on the necklace and the wish will come true. The wish must be made as you are moving the chain hook or clasp to the back of your neck.

🌿 Deirdre Daly, Wantagh, New York

When you see a moving hay truck, make a wish and shut your eyes. If you do not open them until the hay truck is gone, you get your wish. If you look at it again, you lose your wish. (I got my first bra this way.)

🌿 Kathie Friedley, Sussex, New Jersey

The next time you take a walk or drive in the country, remember this: If you meet, pass, or see two piebald horses, one after the other, whisper or think of a wish. Then spit seven times, count to seven, and within seven days you will get your wish.

🌿 Madeline Snow, Fort Lee, New Jersey, as told to her "by an old man in the country."

And quite lastly, a very nice letter and way of wishing from Mrs. John W. Albertsen, Clinton, Washington, who writes:

"My four-year-old and I just finished reading your *Wishing Book*. From the time when I was a little girl, I have known about wishing trees or 'sittin' trees.' They have a thick branch or part of the trunk going at right angles and then up, so that a wisher can sit in it and make a wish by looking at the sky through the branches. Wishing trees are few and far between, but we found one on a hike last Sunday. My daughter wished for a candy bar, and on the way home one for each of us mysteriously appeared in the glove box when her Dad was looking for matches. You should have seen her face!"

A very happy four-year-old. Never, never pass a wishing tree by, but always climb into the "sittin'" seat, look through the branches, and wish. It will come true.

AUTOGRAPH ALBUM RHYMES:
tricky and sassy

HEALTH
HAPPINESS
SUCCESS

I
C
U
R
O
K
2
B
A
+ A
Friend

🌺 Karen Cohn,
Flushing, New York

🌺 Regina Camplese,
Somerville, Massachusetts

O U Q T, I A B U

🌺 Collected by Susan Niemiera from Gene
Kaczmarek, Perth Amboy, New Jersey

U R 2
Good 2 B
4 Got 10

🌺 Beverly, Sussex, New Jersey

Love
Luck
Lollipops

Love
Luck
Laughter

🌺 Mary Kay, Pittsburgh, Pennsylvania

I N V U

G U R A Q T

My ♡ 👖 4 U

I came
all
the
way
down
to
say
hello !

🌺 Darlene, Norwalk, Connecticut

200

I'm the girl from the country, I'm the girl from the town. I'm the girl who spoiled your autograph book by writing round and round.

🌿 Mary Jane Hueber,
Belmont, Massachusetts

I 🚗 cry
I 🚗 laugh
I 🚗 sign
My 🚗 graph

🌿 Deborah Whitley, Potomac, Maryland

Many people write up, And many people write down, But I'd like to be different and write around... Many people write around...

🌿 Barbara Frondel,
Belmont, Massachusetts

LET'S GO AROUND TOGETHER?

🌿 From the autograph album of Betsey Brawner, Chevy Chase, Maryland, 1968, collected
by Sandy Bell

Around this page I've searched a lot to plant this sweet forget-me-not.

🌷 Mary Egan, Dorchester, Massachusetts

A RING IS ROUND AND HAS NO END. SO IS MY FRIENDSHIP FOR YOU MY FRIEND *

🌷 Irene Garrity, Pennsauken, New Jersey

"You must have been a beautiful baby."—
What happened?

    🌺 Hope Miller, East Meadow, New York

Date:

Pay to the order of (Person's name)
The sum of Health, Wealth and Happiness

(Your name)

    🌺 Hope Miller, East Meadow, New York

**Take the road to success
And drive carefully**

    🌺 Hope Miller, East Meadow, New York

204

YOURS TILL, OR DATED UNTIL

Yours till meatballs bounce

Yours till the bed spreads

Yours till the bed springs

Yours till sugar bowls

Yours till the cookie crumbles

Yours till the board walks

Yours till comic strips

Yours till the belly buttons

Yours till the banana peels

Yours till Bob Hopes

Yours till Long Island Sounds

Yours till the apples turnover

Yours till the U.S. drinks Canada dry

Yours till curlers or bobby pins get sick from riding permanent waves

Yours till the living room dies

Yours till the dogwood barks at the pussy willows

Yours till you see the wood work

Yours till soda pops

Yours till Web stirs (Webster's dictionary)

Yours till Bob loses Hope

Yours till Bear Mountain has cubs

Yours till the mouth of the Mississippi
  puts on lipstick

Yours till the pillowcase is solved

Yours till the catfish has kittens

Yours till bacon strips

Yours till side walks

Yours till George Burns

Yours till Victor Matures

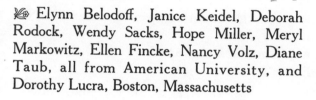

    🦋 Elynn Belodoff, Janice Keidel, Deborah
Rodock, Wendy Sacks, Hope Miller, Meryl
Markowitz, Ellen Fincke, Nancy Volz, Diane
Taub, all from American University, and
Dorothy Lucra, Boston, Massachusetts

Roses are blue,
Violets are red,
If you believe this,
You're sick in the head.

    🦋 From Betsey Brawner's autograph album,
Chevy Chase, Maryland

G. I. Haircut
G. I. Hat
G. I. This, and
G. I. That
G. I. Like you,
G. I. Do,
G. I. Hope you like me, too.

    🦋 Andrea Brown, contributed to her auto-
graph album by Michele Proia, Washington,
D.C.

I wish I had your picture,
It would be very nice,
I'd hang it in the attic
To scare away the mice.

   Susan Blumenfeld, Oceanside, New York

My house is situated near a lake.
Drop in sometime.

   Meryl Green, Forest Hills, New York, from
   her junior high autograph album, JHS 218,
   Queens, New York

Don't go to London,
Don't go to France,
Stay in New York
And give the boys a chance.

Dee El
Oh You
Oh See
Gee Kay
(Up and down it spells Good Luck)

Roses are red,
Violets are blue,
Now you know your flowers.

   Cindy Gross, Passaic, New Jersey

Roses are red,
Violets are blue,
Sugar is sweet,
And so are you!

But . . .

The roses are wilted,
The violets are dead,
The sugar bowl's empty,
And so is your head!

   🥀 Lydia Bloom, New York City

In sixth grade, someone wrote this in my
autograph album:

Roses are red,
Violets are green,
Your ears are cute,
But there's nothing between!

   🥀 Michael Elkisch, New York City

If water is luck,
I wish you the Pacific Ocean.

I wish I were a grapefruit,
And here's the reason why,
When you came to eat me,
I'd squirt you in the eye.

   🥀 Hope Miller, East Meadow, New York

Here's to you and here's to me,
May we never disagree,
But if we do, the heck with you!
And here's to me!

   🥀 Barbara Mitchell, Kingston, Pennsylvania

I am 4 U
B cause U R A
Q
T

🌸 Audrey Lee, River Edge, New Jersey

May your life be like arithmetic:
Joys +	**(Added)**
Sorrows —	**(Subtracted)**
Happiness ✕	**(Multiplied)**
Love (un) ÷	**(Undivided)**

🌸 Irene Garrity, Pennsauken, New Jersey

**On this page of pearly white,
I got hungry and took a bite.**

🌸 Randy Stone, Paramus, New Jersey

FUNEX?
S, VFX,
FUNEM?
S, VFM.
O. K. MNX.

Do you want it interpreted? Have you any eggs? Yes, we have eggs. Have you any ham? Yes, we have ham. OK, ham and eggs.

CDB? DBSABZB.

Interpreted again? See the bee? The bee is a busy bee.

> ✍ Both collected by Mitchell Stein, Erdenheim, Pennsylvania, from Marilyn Hawrys, Brightwater, New York

Ess You See See EEE ESS ESS
(S U C C E S S)

> ✍ Elynn Belodoff, East Meadow, New York, from her father's sixth grade autograph album

4 lines from a lazy poet _____
_____
_____
_____

> ✍ Aimee J. Ornstein, Long Beach, New York

And this nice one:

From someone
Who likes to remember
Someone too nice
Too forget.

> ✍ Beth Barton, Clarks Green, Pennsylvania, and given to her by Sheila Swan, Lincoln, Rhode Island

Life is like a game of cards:

When you're in love, it's ♡

When you're engaged, it's ◇

When you're married, it's ♣

When you're dead, it's ⛏

Climb the ladder of
Success and you will
Reach your goal.
   It's a long trip,
   But you'll make it.

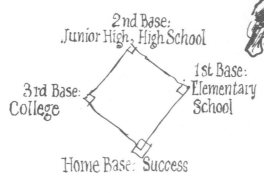

2nd Base:
Junior High, High School

1st Base:
Elementary
School

3rd Base:
College

Home Base: Success

I hope you hit a Home Run!

🌿 The above three from Susan Novinsky,
Freeport, New York

U R
2 Good
2 B
4 Real!

🌿 Susanne Roxbury, McLean, Virginia

Fold right side of page page back — before reading

For girls only

↓ You dirty boy, you had to look. Now you'll kiss the owner of this book.

For pretty girls only.   You're conceited!

For dirty girls only.   Use soap!

Open this page, and you will see the brightest ship of the ocean sea!   Sorry! It sank.

For girls only.   You're a girl? (Boys will invariably be tricked into looking.)

For sweet people only.   Candy.

Don't open until Xmas.   My, my, time sure does fly!

The facts of life.   There is no Easter bunny. Santa told me.

Randy Stone, Paramus, New Jersey; Marcy Devine, Tolland, Connecticut; Kristin Smith, Garden City, New York

Children's Beliefs

MONSTERS IN THE NIGHT
(NOT REAL ONES, OF COURSE)

"I asked a seven-year-old what she was afraid of and she said 'To leave the closet door open, because Dracula would come in and bite my neck.' "

> Sharon Greenstein, Long Beach, New York, from an elementary school youngster at East Meadow, New York

"Monsters were always hiding under the bed at night, just waiting to get at you. In order to be safe, you had to tuck yourself underneath the blankets so that none of your appendages (arms, legs) stuck out over the side of the bed. Even your head had to be well covered. If you allowed one toe to hang over the edge, you could be sure you would soon feel the cold, wet tongue of some wild animal, or the clammy, slimy hand of some monster from the deep."

> Brenda Barth, Clarksburg, West Virginia

"Witches, ghosts, monsters, and wild animals under the bed cannot harm you if you don't see them. You must therefore sleep facing the wall for safety."

 Rob Stirling, Oswego, New York

"If your arm hung over your bed at night, it would be gone in the morning as the monster underneath your bed ate it."

 Bill LaFleur, Fairhaven, New Jersey

"Demons that dwell in dark closets bite off the toes of naughty children."

 Barry Spevack, Westbury, New York

"If you sleep with your feet toward the door, you'll die during the night, because 'The Spirits' can come in and drag you out by the feet. This is especially true if you're older, because it's easier for 'The Spirits' to carry you out."

 Eve Wright, Garrison, New York

"When I was young, I believed that if I stuck my feet or arms over the side of my bed, snakes would get me. The bed was my security."

🌿 John Wilson, Honolulu, Hawaii

This is a game and not really anything to be afraid of. Actually, none of these beliefs should make you or your little sister or brother afraid. They are just shivery imaginings. This is the bedtime game:

Jump from one bed to another, and if you fall between the beds, there is water with sharks in it, and you die. (Or you bang your knee or head on the floor. Make it to the other bed!)

🌿 Sharon Greenstein, Long Beach, New York

"When I was a kid, I'd be afraid to step on bugs or spiders for fear that their ghosts would come back to haunt me in the night."

    🌿 Sandra Lundy, Wynnewood, Pennsylvania. Be kind to little bugs. They haven't hurt you!

"When I was around five or six, I always used to run and jump into bed, because I didn't want the Bogie Man to bite my feet. In fact, I would start in my brother's bedroom to increase my speed into my bed."

    🌿 Tamlyn Perry, Yarmouth, Maine

"When getting into bed, I still jump in to avoid getting my feet caught by the Bogey Man, tiger, or snakes which have always lived under there."

    🌿 Ellen Faryna, Perry, New York

"I used to believe that there was an alligator under my bed waiting to catch my foot and pull me under the bed, so I always took a running leap to get in. Once in the bed, I had to stay curled up at the top because there were monkeys under the sheets at the foot of the bed waiting to grab my toes."

    🌿 Leslie Peak, Philadelphia, Pennsylvania

Nanci Isenberg of Marblehead, Massachusetts, had two means of protecting herself against these imaginary ghoulies and ghosties:

One: Touching the floor on each side of the bed will ward off anything that comes to "get you" in the night.

Two: Touching yourself on each shoulder with your right hand before going to sleep will protect you from anything that could "get you" in your sleep.

And this is entirely "explainable." Very little children do not or cannot understand everything that makes the world go around. How can they understand an airplane and why it stays up? Or an automobile and why it goes? And in this case a toilet. What makes a toilet work? Little children—very little children—have no understanding of the mechanism of a flush toilet. They have no idea of a machine, so . . .

"As children we were always frightened to sit on the toilet unless mother was nearby, because there was a little man who lived there and waited for small children." (Mothers are very, very necessary. You know that, don't you?)

       Virginia Towsey, Washington, D.C.

And of course:

If you are a bad boy, the goblins will take you away.

       Barry Spevack of Long Island, who picked up that certain truth from a 2nd grader in Washington, D.C.

TWO BEDTIME PRAYERS

To be rid of all this nightime scariness, here
are two wonderful prayers, both of them very
old, but both used today everywhere:

Now I lay me down to sleep,
I pray the Lord my soul to keep;
If I should die before I wake,
I pray the Lord my soul to take.
God bless Mommy, Daddy, Nancy, Ken,
    Steve, and Martha.

  🥀 Linda Coleman, Boston, Massachusetts

Now I lay me down to sleep,
I pray the Lord my soul to keep;
Watch me through the dark, dark night,
And wake me in the morning light.

  🥀 Jamie Rothstein, Woodmere, New York

And:

I see the first star,
The first star sees me,
God bless the first star
And my family.

  🥀 Susan Novinsky, Freeport, New York

GOD

Here are three very pleasant beliefs that six-year-olds have about God, collected by two of my students:

If you climb a mountain, you can see God.

> Mark Seides, Long Beach, New York

God is like my Daddy except He is bigger.

God can frown like my Daddy and smile like my Mommy.

> E. Neil Norris, Washington, D.C.

THE TOOTH FAIRY

The tooth fairy is part and parcel of almost everyone's childhood.

"We were told that we should make a wish and put the tooth under our pillow. If the tooth was gone in the morning and replaced by a coin, we had been good and would get our wish. But if the tooth was still there, then we had been bad and would not get our wish—or the dime or quarter, depending upon which tooth. Front teeth were usually worth more."

> Margie Stegman, Norwalk, Connecticut, learned from her mother in Wilmington, Delaware, in the late 1950s

"When our oldest child lost her first tooth, she didn't want to put it under her pillow because she didn't want 'that tooth fairy flying around her room at night.' The girl next door who baby-sits for us told us that in her family they drop the tooth in a glass of water anywhere in the house where it can be found by the tooth fairy. Our other children haven't minded the presence of the tooth fairy in their rooms, but our oldest child still prefers the glass of water."

Mary Campbell, Chevy Chase, Maryland

"When one of my teeth came out, I put it under my pillow. If the good fairy came that night, a quarter would be under my pillow in the morning. I lost a lot of teeth but only got two quarters."

Mitchell Stein, Erdenheim, Pennsylvania

What do the fairies do with the teeth they take away when they leave a dime?

They build their fences with them. Therefore they are only interested in clean teeth!

Joy Huston, Sydney, Australia

MOTHER NATURE

Two of my students at American University —Janet Disken of New Haven, Connecticut, and Karen Cohn of Flushing, New York— collected beliefs about Mother Nature from second, third, fourth, and fifth grade youngsters. They also collected the children's beliefs about The Man in the Moon and The Tooth Fairy. I'll give you a couple of those following Mother Nature, but now—Mother Nature. And these were collected from children at two elementary schools: The Mann Elementary School in Washington, D.C., and the Miller Elementary School in Plymouth, Michigan. The descriptions were given to Janet and Karen in writing by the children.

Here goes with Mother Nature:

Mother Nature is a person. She can make rain and sunny, too. It's not nice to fool Mother Nature. POW!

> Valerie Calhoun
> Second Grade, Mann Elementary

Mother Nature is flowers and bees and trees. She makes Spring and Summer.

> Cairn
> Second Grade, Mann Elementary

She is a lady. She makes animals have their babys in the Spring. And makes rain, snow, and the sun.

🌺 Theodore Calhoun
Third Grade, Mann Elementary

Mother Nature is white and old. She is little and ugly. She is 90. She makes the trees grow and makes it snow.

🌺 Tony
Fourth Grade, Miller Elementary

Mother nature is short. She has green leaves for her body. For her hair she has green grass. She is going steady with the Jolly Green Giant.

🌺 Sue
Fourth Grade, Miller Elementary

I think Mother nature has long black hair and her fingers are different colors, so that anything she touches turns that color. She wears a colorful dress. She is the same size as the grass. Her face is green. She wears her hair in pony tails.

Chris Brennan
Fourth Grade, Miller Elementary

Mother Nature is the head of all the animals and trees. She looks like a little old lady who has ringlets all over her face. She limps a little, so sometimes she uses a cane.

Rhonda Walters
Fifth Grade, Miller Elementary

Mother Nature is always something different. When she wants flowers, she turns herself into a flower and then she blows her seeds. If she wants to have more deer, she turns herself into a deer and has some babies.

Linda Vaught
Fifth Grade, Miller Elementary

Mother Nature is a dog. Every time she barks, she'll make it snow or rain.

    ❦ Mack Nash
    Fifth Grade, Miller Elementary

Mother Nature is about thirty million years old. She was around a long time. She still works, but she's slowed down.

    ❦ John Shannon
    Fifth Grade, Miller Elementary

Mother Nature is a spirit. She comes out once a year. She wears lacey white snow for her gown. The willow tree branches are her hair. The wind is her echo. In the summer she's always growing. But in the winter she goes out of control.

    ❦ Michelle Clancy
    Fifth Grade, Miller Elementary

THE TOOTH FAIRY AGAIN

And now for Tooth Fairy descriptions from the same youngsters:

The tooth fairy is your Mom on her tip toes walking in your bedroom. She takes your teeth and waits until she has enough for false teeth.

> Linda Vaught
> Fifth Grade, Miller Elementary

The tooth fairy is blue and she has the prettiest teeth. She is small, has wings, and her house is made of decade (decayed) teeth. The door is made of white teeth.

> Grace Srullard
> Fifth Grade, Miller Elementary

The tooth fairy is a old lady that takes teeth. She wears a hard hat and uses a jackhammer. She takes teeth because she can't afford to buy a pair of dencers (dentures).

> John Shannon
> Fifth Grade, Miller Elementary

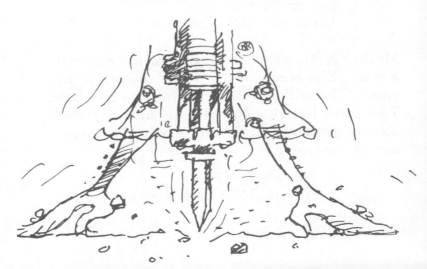

The tooth fairy is your mother or your father. When your tooth comes out and you put it under your pillow, then your mother or your father will take it out from your pillow and throw it in the trash, and put some money under your pillow. And then the next day you will see some money. And then you will spend it on the ice cream man. The End.

🌿 Phyllis Young
Third Grade, Mann Elementary

AND THE MAN IN THE MOON?

The Man on the Moon is small. He is green with a fish bowl over his head. He has big feet, small hands. He lives in a house made of green cheese. He has a playground. The slide is gone, because it was made out of green cheese. He ate it.

🌿 Tina
Fourth Grade, Miller Elementary

228

The Man in the Moon is a little thing with big fangs. He eats moon rocks and left over Tang. He makes tunals (tunnels) and digs for cheese.

   🌙 John Shannon
   Fifth Grade, Miller Elementary

The Man on the Moon is mean. He is very mean. He takes the rocks and throws them at the space ship and gets mad. (There follows a drawing of the "Mad man on the moon.")

   🌙 Chris Bartlett
   Fourth Grade, Miller Elementary

Aren't they delightful? What do you believe the Man in the Moon looks like? And Mother Nature?

IF YOU SWALLOW A GRAPEFRUIT SEED

In an effort to keep young children from swallowing prune pits, daily doses of orange seeds, fingernails, and other normally inedible matter, mothers and grandmothers have made up wondrous tales to alarm and excite their youngsters.

"I was told by my Mom that if you eat the seeds of an apple, you'll grow an apple tree in your stomach."

   🌙 Nancy Gendler, South Hampstead, New York

"If you bite your fingernails and eat them, potatoes will grow in your ears."

🌹 Linda Ross (from her family), Belmar, New Jersey

"If you eat the seeds in grapes, grapevines will grow in your stomach and come out your ears."

🌹 Victoria Schaeffer (from her mother), Wyomissing, Pennsylvania

"If you swallow a grapefruit or orange seed, it will grow in your stomach, and if you swallow chewing gum, your insides will stick together."

🌹 Fran Goodman (from her mother), Mount Vernon, New York

"If you drink too much water, you will get frogs in your stomach."

🌹 Helen Metaxas, Margate, New Jersey, and Karen Coburn, Queens, New York

"Food eaten before grace is said will rot in your stomach."

🌹 Cynthia Barnett (from her aunt), Decatur, Illinois

230

IF YOU EAT BANANAS

But then, of course, there are small beliefs told the child in an effort to induce him to eat "what is good for him," and spinach to give one strength (Popeye). Anyhow, a few:

"If you eat a lot of green vegetables, you won't get wrinkles on your elbows."

> 🥬 Mitchell Stein (from his mother), Erdenheim, Pennsylvania

If you eat bananas, you will grow tall."

> 🥬 Helen Metaxas, Margate, New Jersey, and Karen Coburn, Queens, New York

Fish is brain food.

Eating oatmeal puts hair on your chest.

> 🥬 Susan Burns, Derby, Vermont

ITCHES

If your nose itches, it means either that company is coming or that you have a rip in your pants.

🌿 Ronnie Aronchick, Bradley Beach, New Jersey

If your right nostril itches, it means that someone is thinking about you, but if your left nostril itches, it means you are going to get a spanking.

🌿 Margaret Trytell, New York City

SNEEZING

Some people believe that every time you sneeze three times in succession you lose one minute of your life. Could be, but how would you ever know?

🌿 Also from Ronnie Aronchick

If you sneeze upon waking, that is, before you get out of bed in the morning, you're bound to fight with the first person you see.

🌿 Elizabeth Miller, Pittsburgh, Pennsylvania

FUNNY FACES AND CROSSED EYES

If you make a funny face and the wind changes, your face will stay that way.

> 🌿 Ralph Lewis, Morgantown, West Virginia

My grandfather told me never to make a face at anyone because it would become frozen on my face, and then I'd have to walk around the rest of my life like that.

> 🌿 Nancy Gendler, from her grandfather in Salt Lake City, Utah

My mother told me never to pull my bottom eyelids down, because if someone slapped me on the back, they would surely stay that way.

> 🌿 Kathie Friedley, from her mother, Dorothy Friedley, Sussex, New Jersey

If someone slaps you on the back while your eyes are crossed, they'll remain that way for the rest of your life.

> 🌿 Nancy Greenspan, Larchmont, New York

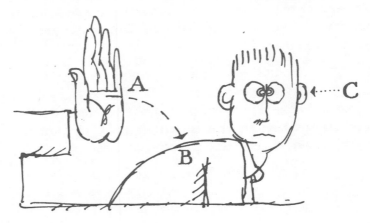

My sister used to tell me never to cross my eyes in bed, because I might fall asleep that way and not be able to uncross them when I woke up.

🌿 Eleni Nichols, Annapolis, Maryland

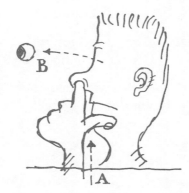

EYES

Don't pick your nose or your eyes will fall out.

🌿 Deborah Whitley, Potomac, Maryland

My brother-in-law, Mike, insists that if you sneeze with your eyes open, your eyeballs will pop out. As yet, no one has tried to prove him wrong.

🌿 Arnold Stone, from Mike Sharp, Baltimore, Maryland

If you watch too much T.V., your eyes will fall out.

🌿 Bruce Chase, Hackensack, New Jersey

Try to make a child stop crying: "Don't cry or the color in your eyes will fade."

🌿 Sharon Dill, Somerville, New Jersey

FINGERNAILS

If you bite your nails, worms will crawl out of them.

> Collected by Jane Leff, New Rochelle, New York, from a child in a class she was student-teaching.

If you bite your fingernails, you will always be poor and you will have bad dreams.

> Helen Metaxas, Margate, New Jersey, and Karen Coburn, Queens, New York

THUMB SUCKING

"When I was home from the university for Spring vacation, my little sister, Bari Lyn Barton, who was four was trying not to suck her thumb. She was having a terrible time and was very cranky. I asked her why she was behaving that way. She told me that it was because she couldn't suck her thumb. I asked her why, and she replied: 'If I suck my thumb, I'll turn into a bird.' She told me that our brother-in-law, Joel, told her that."

> Beth Barton, Clarks Green, Pennsylvania

EARS

When your ears pop, another angel has just gotten his wings.

> 🌸 Barbara Shapiro, Kansas City, Missouri

Put nothing in your ears but your elbows.

> 🌸 Susan Batoff, Wynwood, Pennsylvania

"If I wash behind my ears too much, they'll fall off."

> 🌸 Eliza Novick, New Jersey, remembered from her childhood

HOT AND COLD WATER

"I used to think that the reservoir was divided in half, one half cold water and the other half hot, and that if I turned on the hot water faucet the water would come from the hot side."

> 🌸 Wendy Sacks, Newton Centre, Massachusetts

HOW TO GET A BOYFRIEND

A tan before April 10th means you'll get a boyfriend before the end of the summer.

🌺 Lori Brudnick, New York

CAREFUL!

If you pick the lint out of your belly button, you will die.

🌺 Rob Stirling, Oswego, New York

TROLLS

Kiss the ground before you walk over a bridge or the trolls will get you.

🌺 Deborah Whitley, Potomac, Maryland, remembered from her childhood in North Carolina

THE LITTLE MAN INSIDE THE PEANUT

A little man lives inside each peanut. You can see him if you split the peanut correctly. Actually, only his head is visible: he has a moustache, a beard, and a conical hat and looks like an elf.

    🖋 Nancy Van Alstine, Bethesda, Maryland, who reports it as a family belief. Maybe it's true. I haven't tried it yet. You try.

YAHUDI

"Every time you open up the refrigerator door, the light is turned on by a little man named Yahudi."

    🖋 Barry Spevack, Westbury, New York, as told to him by "a little friend on Long Island."

NEW YEAR'S DAY

On New Year's Day, if a light-haired person enters the house first, you'll have good luck, but if a dark-haired person is the first to enter, you'll have bad luck.

> 🌿 Linda Ross, Belmar, New Jersey

Always make sure a man enters the house after midnight on January 1 to insure good luck to the house and its people throughout the coming year. My grandmother would send my grandfather out the back door to have him enter the front door if she was expecting a woman visitor the next day.

> 🌿 Claudia Marino, from her grandmother, Mrs. Irene Wells, Baltimore, Maryland

On New Year's Day, if you are the first man (or boy) to enter a house, you will have good luck for the rest of the year.

> 🌿 Sharon Nash, Washington, D.C.

Put a piece of parsley on the bottom shelf of your refrigerator on New Year's Day, and you will never be without money during the year.

> 🌿 Matrice Green, Washington, D.C. from a friend in Durham, North Carolina

CHRISTMAS EVE

"My mother remembers this practice as a child, so it must be fairly old. Every Christmas Eve at midnight, everyone including the children waits up to see if our dogs will talk at midnight. It's great fun trying to guess what they will say."

> 🌺 Mary Michele Roach, from her mother, Frances C. Roach, in Connecticut. The belief that animals talk at midnight on Christmas Eve is an old, old one, at least seven hundred years old.

ST. ANTHONY

"I went to a Catholic grammar and high school, and the nuns always told us that if we ever lost anything, we should pray to St. Anthony: St. Anthony, St. Anthony, please come around. Something is lost and cannot be found."

> 🌺 Linda Ross, Belmar, New Jersey

WHEN NEAR A BEE

When near a bee, say "Bread and Butter" three times very quickly, so that he won't sting you.

Barbara Lee, West Yarmouth, Massachusetts

LEAVE THE FROG ALONE

If you take a frog out of a pond, the pond will dry up.

Richard Jaszczult, Alexandria, Virginia, but learned from a housekeeper in West Virginia. Frogs are, of course, very useful, since they eat mosquitoes and other insects—and they should be left alone.

CRY BEFORE DINNER

If you laugh or sing before breakfast, you'll cry before dinner.

Deborah Whitley, Potomac, Maryland

STEPPING OVER A PERSON

If you step over a child or even an older person, that person won't grow. If you should happen to step over a person by accident, step back over that person in order to cancel out the bad effects of the first step.

> Sandra Lundy, Wynnewood, Pennsylvania, and learned from her parents. This is a belief which teaches "Safety First." You might hurt the child or trip and hurt yourself. Many of these "superstitions" make good sense. Some do not, of course, but are purely for fun.

SLEEP NORTH-SOUTH

If you sleep north-south, you'll grow tall and thin. If you sleep east-west, you'll grow short and fat.

> Ellen Faryna, Perry, New York, from her mother

WATCH IT!

If you are punished on Sunday, you will be punished every day of the week.

> Helen Metaxas, Margate, New Jersey, and Karen Coburn, Queens, New York

DON'T RISK A FALL

If you climb through a window, you won't grow.

> 🌿 Wendy Cagen, Swampscott, Massachusetts, from her grandmother

NIGHTMARES

If you eat a banana before you go to sleep, you will have nightmares.

> 🌿 Amy Singer, who heard this from a friend from Barrington, Rhode Island

If you sleep with your socks on, you will have nightmares.

> 🌿 Jerry Malitz, Brooklyn, New York from his grandmother

KEEP THE FLOORS CLEAN

Don't wear boots or rubbers indoors or you will get a headache.

> 🌿 Judy Deutsch, Syosset, New York, from her grandmother

KISS A COW

If a child kisses a cow before the child is a year old, it will never get whooping cough.

> Elizabeth Miller, Pittsburgh, Pennsylvania, a belief from the Pennsylvania Dutch

BAT BALDNESS

If a bat sits on your head, you will go bald.

> Virginia Towsey, Washington, D.C.

DREAMS

If you dream of the same thing three times in succession, it will positively come true.

> Eve Wright, Garrison, New York, from her grandmother

GIVE HER THE NEEDLES

"When I was young and unhappy, my brother-in-law used to pretend he was a doctor and give me the needles. This was actually a poking of fingers in my side to make me laugh. I now use this on my nieces and younger sister."

> Linda Lukow, Jericho, New York

Proverbs
and
Proverbial Speech

246

Today's oak...

It's an interesting thing that proverbs (and proverbial speech) exist in every family. Ask your mother or father to give you a proverb. They will. And keep your ears open all day: your schoolteacher, the grocery man, the mailman . . . you'll hear proverbs. Let's see: "You don't get something for nothing." "Take care of the pennies and the dollars will take care of themselves." "A stitch in time saves nine." "Never put off till tomorrow . . . ." You'll hear them. Here are a few from some of my students who heard them from their mothers and grandmothers. You've heard a lot of them. But just to remind you:

. . . as loud as a two-dollar watch.

> 🌿 Marie Kisner, who heard her father use the expression, San Antonio, Texas

Today's oak is yesterday's nut that held its ground.

> 🌿 Marie Kisner, who reported it as a sign in a store window in Arlington, Virginia

Success comes in cans,
Failure comes in can'ts.

> 🐝 Jamie Rothstein, Woodmere, New York, who learned this from his mother

If you earn a dime, save a penny.

> 🐝 From Deborah Whitley, who learned it from her great-grandmother in Tennessee

It doesn't matter whether you win or lose: it's how you play the game.

> 🐝 Bill Chuck, New York City, from his father. Very good advice, by the way.

A wise man learns from others' experiences.
An intelligent man learns from his own.
A fool never learns.

> 🐝 Doris Indyke, who had this from her mother in New York. Quite true, of course. Mothers are usually right.

Grass doesn't grow on a busy street.

> 🐝 Barbara Zeller, Hillside, New Jersey, who said that her "future father-in-law" stated this to explain baldness. Could be.

Tomorrow never comes, because when it does, it's today.

> 🖋 Nancy Gendler, Baldwin, New York

The most lost day of all is the day you do not laugh.

> 🖋 E. Neil Norris from her great-grandmother in Knoxville, Tennessee

If you don't eat it,
It can't turn to fat.

> 🖋 Claudia F. Marino from her mother, Mrs. Gladys Napora, Laurel, Maryland

and another:

A moment on the lips, a lifetime on the hips!

(I know you like candy, but you don't want to eat all that much, do you?)

A thousand mile journey begins with the first step.

> 🖋 Sharon Weber, Brooklyn, New York. In other words, take the first step and get started on what you are about to do. Don't wait!

Too many cooks spoil the broth.

All that glitters is not gold.

> 🌾 Jane McAuliffe, Glencoe, Illinois

The morning hours have gold in their mouth.

> 🌾 Wendy Cagen, Swampscott, Massachusetts. (Isn't that beautiful?)

When a task is first begun,
Never leave it 'til it's done.

> 🌾 Susan Gilbert, Overland Park, Kansas

The hand that rocks the cradle rules the world.

A smooth sea never made a skilled sailor.

> 🌾 Collected by Cathy Robertson, Oyster Bay, New York, from Mildred Hale, Durand, Michigan

He who steals what isn't his'n,
Must pay back or go to prison.

> 🌾 Susanne Roxbury from her mother, Lucy Roxbury, McLean, Virginia

Cheaters never win.

> 🌾 Nancy Gendler, from friends at camp, Monroe, New York

The same heat that melts the butter hardens the egg.

🌺 Margaret Trytell, New York City

The greatest business in the world is to have a business of your own. If you cannot find a business of your own . . . make it your business to leave other people's business alone.

🌺 Martrice Green, Washington, D.C.

What will be will be.

🌺 Linda Lukow, Jericho, New York, who says that she has heard it from her mother "as long as I can remember."

Better safe than sorry.

The bigger they are, the harder they fall.

Rich or poor . . .
It's nice to have money.

🌺 Bill Chuck, New York City

Nothing worth coming by comes easily.

🌺 Gail Silverman, New York City

Just remember:
When you are not practicing,
Somebody, somewhere, is,
And when the two of you meet,
He will win.

🌺 John A. Lawton, Lebanon, New Jersey

As men dare, so men fare.

> 🖙 A very wonderful proverb, learned by Mary
> Balicki, Chicopee, Massachusetts, from her
> father

And also from her:

Many a truth is said in jest.

You're only as big as your heart is.

A bird in the hand is worth two in the bush.

And a couple of parodies:

A bird in the hand is warm.

A bird in the hand makes blowing your nose difficult.

> 🖙 Robin Cohen, New York City

People in glass houses shouldn't throw stones.

> 🖙 Sharon Scheinthal, New Hyde Park, New
> York. (Do you know what that means? Ask
> your teacher.)

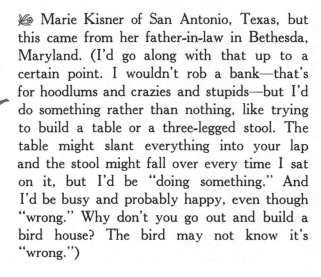

Do something—even if it's wrong.

🎐 Marie Kisner of San Antonio, Texas, but this came from her father-in-law in Bethesda, Maryland. (I'd go along with that up to a certain point. I wouldn't rob a bank—that's for hoodlums and crazies and stupids—but I'd do something rather than nothing, like trying to build a table or a three-legged stool. The table might slant everything into your lap and the stool might fall over every time I sat on it, but I'd be "doing something." And I'd be busy and probably happy, even though "wrong." Why don't you go out and build a bird house? The bird may not know it's "wrong.")

What goes up must come down.

🎐 Louis Leventhal, Long Island. (That applies to Newton's law of gravity, to the stock market, and to a cheese soufflé.)

Bad luck often brings good.

🎐 Claudia F. Marino who learned this from her grandmother, Mrs. Irene Wells of Baltimore, Maryland. Now just take a moment (by yourself, or at dinner with your family) to figure out those things which have brought good out of bad—or what must have seemed to be totally bad to begin with, and then which brought some good.

The sheep and the wolf are not agreed upon a definition of the word "Liberty."

🎐 E. Terris Devereaux who heard it from his father in Connecticut

Always laugh when you can: it is cheap medicine.

Where there's a will, there's a way.

>  Barbara Zeller, Hillside, New Jersey. Of course!

Remember the 2 Ps:
Patience and Perseverance!

> Ann Markunas from her grandmother, Maggie Lyter, Dauphin, Pennsylvania. "She's been saying this for as long as I can remember."

If the shoe fits, wear it.

> Margaret Trytell who learned it from Miss Graves, Rowayton, Connecticut. If you don't know what that means, ask your favorite uncle.

Life is a bowl of cherries,
But watch out for the pits!

> Fran Goodman, and acquired from Dora Greenspan, Bronx, New York

If wishes were horses, beggars would ride.

You make your bed, and you lie in it.

> 🐝 Suzan Marie Graham, Bloomfield, New Jersey. Again, you may need your favorite uncle.

Always let sleeping dogs lie.

> 🐝 Anne Mendelsohn, Bethesda, Maryland. If you wake him, he might bite you. In other words, don't hunt for trouble.

If life hands you a lemon, make lemonade!

> 🐝 E. Neil Norris, Washington, D.C.

All we want from our children is joy and happiness.

> 🐝 Jay Bass, Bethesda, Maryland. Give it to your mother and father. It's so easy, and they've done so much for you—haven't they?

SHE'S SO SKINNY...

A part of proverbial speech is the colorful description of people. For example, instead of saying "He's dumb," it's more colorful and also quite common to say, "He's too dumb to come in out of the rain." Well then, here are a dozen or so given me by my students, and all of them quite colorful. And you can believe that all of them have been used!

He'd leave his head on his pillow in the morning if it weren't attached to his shoulders.

🌸 Jay Bass, Bethesda, Maryland

He has the tact of a wild boar.

🌸 Eleni Nichols, Annapolis, Maryland

Of a smart person: He's got more brains than a cat's got hairs.

🌸 Mitchell Stein, Erdenheim, Pennsylvania

He'd argue with a signpost.

🌸 Marie Kisner, San Antonio, Texas

My boyfriend once told me: "You're so skinny, you could turn sideways, and no one would see you. In fact, you're so thin, you could walk in between raindrops."

🐝 Martrice Green, Washington, D.C.

She's so skinny she has to jump around in the shower to get wet.

🐝 Rhonda Madow, Marblehead, Massachusetts

He's so skinny that when he turns to the side and sticks out his tongue, he looks like a zipper.

🐝 Doris Indyke, Rockville Center, New York

She's so thin the scale goes down when she gets on it.

🐝 Sharon Ladenheim, Stamford, Connecticut

My cousin is so fat that when she goes to take a shower, she uses up all the hot water before her toes get wet.

🐝 Sandra Lundy, Wynnewood, Pennsylvania

She's so short she's liable to get lost in the grass.

🐝 Sharon Ladenheim, Stamford, Connecticut

You look like a barefooted goose walking in a snowstorm!

🐝 Deborah Whitley, Potomac, Maryland, but heard from her father in Tennessee

You're as fluttery as if you'd seen a ghost.

🐛 E. Neil Norris, Washington, D.C., but heard from her mother in Chicago, Illinois

He's dumb enough to gargle with peanut butter.

🐛 Cynthia Barnett, Decatur, Illinois

Of a very shrewd and clever young man:
Putting one over on him is like trying to slip the sun past the rooster.

🐛 Christopher Scully, who picked this up from his father in Sparrowbush, New York

Talking to that fool is like trying to put socks on an octopus.

🐛 Paul Ferber, Verena, New Jersey, but heard from the grandmother of a friend of his from suburban Boston

He chews his gum so loud, it's a shame he can't produce milk!

🐛 Margaret Trytell, New York City

MORE COMPARISONS

Just try once—once only—at dinner or the supper table to come up with as many comparisons as you can. From your mother, father, and anyone else there. I'll bet that you hit fifty. Or more!

All of these come from three students. I didn't ask for them. If I had asked for them from the whole class, there would be pages and pages here. The students are Debbi Carter, Upton, Massachusetts; Linda Coleman, Boston, Massachusetts; and Marie Kisner, San Antonio, Texas.

> Madder than a hornet
> Cute as a button
> Stubborn as a mule
> Ugly as sin
> Slipperier than a greased pig
> Quicker than greased lightning
> Busy as a beaver
> Neat as a pin
> Tall as a beanpole
> Hard as nails
> Crazy as a jaybird
> Don't sit there like a bump on a log
> Noisy as a hog eating shingles

YESTERDAY IS GONE

Think a little bit about these:

Yesterday is gone,
Tomorrow may never come,
Today is here.

🌺 Megan Holbrook, New York

Yesterday's gone, forget it,
Tomorrow's not here yet, don't worry.
Today is here—use it!

🌺 Jo Anne Kessler, Brooklyn, New York

Today is Monday,
Tomorrow's Tuesday,
Next day's Wednesday—
Here's half the week gone and nothin' done
  yet!

🌺 Katherine McManus, Binghamton, New
York, from her great aunt

THESE TWO YOU WILL NOT FORGET

I had no shoes and complained
Until I met a man with no feet.

🐟 Leslie Peak, Philadelphia, Pennsylvania

I wept because I had no shoes . . .
And then I met a man who had no feet.

🐟 David Wildberger, Baltimore, Maryland, from his mother

A THOUGHT

And this can be a serious thought. Now, and later. Consider it. It's nicely stated, which makes it something to remember. Ask your grandmother or grandfather, or keep it to yourself.

I wish I was what I was
When I wished I was what I am now.

🐟 Jane McAuliffe, Glencoe, Illinois

And a very close variant:

I wish I was what I was
Before I wanted to be what I am now.

🐟 Tamlyn Perry, Yarmouth, Maine, which she "picked up from a friend from New Jersey."

Try this one:

"Is" is the was of what shall be.

🍂 Also from Tamlyn Perry

and:

The hurrier I go the behinder I get.

🍂 Eileen Agard, Princeton, Massachusetts

...if you know what I mean

And figure this one out:

I know you believe you understand what you think I said, but I am not sure you realize that what you heard is not what I meant.

🍂 Maggie Miles, Chevy Chase, Maryland

Also:

I waste more time thinking about the time I'm wasting than there is time to waste.

🍂 Barbara Mendelson, Highland Park, Illinois

SOUND ADVICE

"Here's a little poem that has helped many of my friends and me in times of need:

Put up in a place
Where it's easy to see
The cryptic admonishment:
T. T. T.

When you think how exceedingly
Slowly things climb,
Always remember
Things Take Time."

      Beverly Feinstein, Haworth, New Jersey

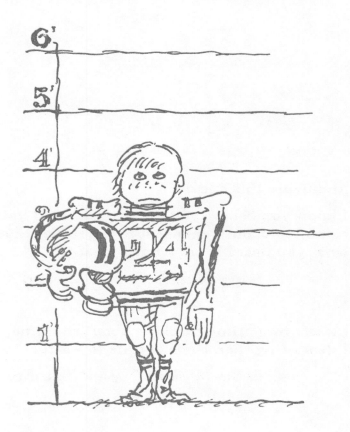

Don't lie,
Or your mother will faint,
And your father will fall
In a bucket of paint.

Take time to be friendly:
It's the road to Happiness.

It's nice to be important,
But it's more important to be nice.

Don't rush: there's always a tomorrow for
your dreams to come true.

Be quick to say "I'm sorry,"
Avoid "I told you so."
Speak freely when your words are praise,
When finding fault, be slow.

If you don't have anything good to say about
anyone,
Then don't say anything at all.

What have you done to help someone today?
A good question: ask it of yourself each
evening.

> Elizabeth McLellan, who comes from Cam-
den, Maine—a beautiful town where the moun-
tains meet the sea—and who heard and learned
these from her mother and father.

School and
Summer Camp Songs
and Cheers

266

SCHOOL AND SUMMER CAMP SONGS

Gray Squirrel

Gray squirrel, gray squirrel,
Swish your bushy tail,
Gray squirrel, gray squirrel,
Swish your bushy tail,
Put a nut between your toes,
Wrinkle up your funny nose,
Gray squirrel, gray squirrel,
Swish your bushy tail.

🍂 Linda Coleman, Washington, D.C.

The Little Skunk

I stuck my head in a little skunk's hole,
And the little skunk said, "Well, bless my
   soul,
Take it out, take it out, take it out,
Remove it!"

I didn't take it out, and the little skunk
   said,
"If you don't take it out, you'll wish you
   were dead.
Take it out, take it out, take it out—
   pssshhh—"
I removed it!

🍂 Brenda Lebowitz, New Rochelle, New York

The Wheels on the Bus Go 'Round

The wheels on the bus go 'round and 'round,
  'round and 'round, 'round and 'round,
The wheels on the bus go 'round and 'round,
  'round and 'round, 'round and 'round,
All through the town.

The horn on the bus goes beep, beep, beep,
Beep, beep, beep, Beep, beep, beep,
The horn on the bus goes beep, beep, beep,
Beep, beep, beep, Beep, beep, beep,
All through the town.

The driver on the bus says "Move on back,
  move on back, move on back,"
The driver on the bus says "Move on back,
  move on back, move on back,"
All through the town.

The kids on the bus go up and down, up
  and down, up and down,
The kids on the bus go up and down, up
  and down, up and down
All through the town.

         Meryl Markowitz, Oceanside, New York.
         They must have driven the bus driver crazy!

Birds in the Wilderness

To be sung with banging of spoons and forks and glasses on the table at lunch and dinner time in the camp dining room:

Here we sit like birds in the wilderness,
Birds in the wilderness, birds in the
   wilderness,
Here we sit like birds in the wilderness
Waiting for our food,
Waiting for our food, waiting for our food,
Here we sit like birds in the wilderness
Waiting for our food.

and when the meal is finished:

Here we sit like birds in the wilderness,
Birds in the wilderness, birds in the
   wilderness,
Here we sit like birds in the wilderness
Waiting to be excused,
Waiting to be excused, waiting to be excused,
Here we sit like birds in the wilderness
Waiting to be excused.

Bobbi Berman, Baltimore, Maryland, from Camp Wohelo, Waynesboro, Pennsylvania

Web-Footed Friends

Be kind to your web-footed friends,
For a duck may be somebody's mother.
Be kind to your friends in the swamp
Where the weather is very, very domp.
You may think that this is the end—
Well, it is!

       ✽ Diane Taub, Plainfield, New Jersey

These next two songs which can continue
endlessly are sung to the tune of Frere Jacques:

We Are Crazy

We are crazy, we are crazy,
We are nuts, we are nuts,
Happy little morons, happy little morons,
Blp, blp, blp; Blp, blp, blp!

Watermelon, Watermelon

Watermelon, watermelon,
How it drips, how it drips,
Up and down your elbow, up and down your
    elbow,
Spit out the pits, spit out the pits:
Pff, pff, pff; Pff, pff, pff!

**And three more endless ones from camp, all
collected by** Denise Miness, Baldwin, New York

Ain't It Great to Be Nuts

Bum, bum, ain't it great to be crazy,
Bum, bum, ain't it great to be nuts—like us?
Bum, bum, ain't it great to be crazy,
Bum, bum, ain't it great to be nuts?

If You're Happy and You Know It

If you're happy and you know it, clap your
hands (clap, clap),
If you're happy and you know it, clap your
hands (clap, clap),
If you're happy and you know it, and you
really want to show it,
If you're happy and you know it, clap your
hands (clap, clap).

For the next two stanzas:

If you're happy and you know it, toot your
horn (toot, toot).
If you're happy and you know it, stamp
your feet (stamp, stamp).

And for the last stanza, all three:

If you're happy and you know it, do all
three (clap, clap, toot, toot, stamp, stamp),
If you're happy and you know it, do all
three (clap, clap, toot, toot, stamp, stamp),
If you're happy and you know it, and you
really want to show it,
If you're happy and you know it, do all
three (clap, clap, toot, toot, stamp, stamp).

This Old Man

This old man, he played one,
He played nick-nack on my drum,
With a nick-nack, paddy-wack
Give a dog a bone,
This old man came rolling home.

A child can count as high as he wants, and the song can go on forever, for example:

Two—shoe; three—knee; four—door; five—hive; six—sticks; seven—up in heaven; eight—gate; nine—spine; ten—pen; and so on indefinitely, or he can start over again with one, two, three, four.

Saw a Rabbit Hopping By

Old man by the window stood,
Looking out into the wood.
Saw a rabbit hopping by,
Knocking at his door.
"Help me! Help me, sir!" he cried,
"Before the hunter shoots me dead!"
"Come inside and stay awhile.
Safely you'll abide."

This song has hand movements:

Old man by the window stood—you draw a window in the air.
Looking out into the wood—put your two hands over your eyes as though you were looking into the distance.
Saw a rabbit hopping by—pretend your hand is the rabbit, and make it hop across in front of you.
Knocking at his door—a rapping or knocking motion.
"Help me! help me, Sir!" he cried—pull back and make a movement to show fright.
"Before the hunter shoots me dead!"—pretend a gun is in your hand and shoot.
"Come inside and stay awhile."—Motion for the rabbit to come in.
"Safely you'll abide."—Pretend you are cradling the rabbit in your arms.

Then repeat the song. The first time you sing it, it is without any hand motions. The second time, don't sing the last line, but use the motion instead. The next time, do the motions for the last two lines instead of the words. And you continue this until the whole thing is a pantomine and there is no singing at all.

🐌 Diane Taub, Plainfield, New Jersey

B–I–N–G–O

This is a summer camp song reported from Pennsylvania, New York, Connecticut, New Jersey, Massachusetts, and all over the lot. You surely know it. The fun part of it is in the changing stanzas. At first, you spell out BINGO completely as you sing it. With the second stanza, you drop the B and "clap" instead. With the third, you drop the B and I, and "clap, clap" instead. And so on until at the end you are not singing any words but simply "clap, clapping" for the five letters. Here we go.

There was a farmer had a dog, and Bingo
  was his name–O,
B–I–N–G–O, B–I–N–G–O, B–I–N–G–O,
And Bingo was his name.

There was a farmer had a dog, and Bingo
  was his name–O,
clap–I–N–G–O, clap–I–N–G–O, clap–I–N–G–O,
And Bingo was his name.

There was a farmer had a dog, and Bingo
  was his name–O,
clap-clap–N–G–O, clap-clap–N–G–O,
  clap-clap–N–G–O,
And Bingo was his name.

There was a farmer had a dog, and Bingo
  was his name–O,
clap-clap-clap–G–O, clap-clap-clap–G–O,
  clap-clap-clap–G–O,
And Bingo was his name.

There was a farmer had a dog, and Bingo
   was his name–O,
clap–clap–clap–clap–O, clap–clap–clap–clap–O,
   clap–clap–clap–clap–O,
And Bingo was his name.

There was a farmer had a dog, and Bingo
   was his name–O,
clap–clap–clap–clap–clap, clap–clap–clap–
   clap–clap, clap–clap–clap–clap–clap,
And Bingo was his name.

He's still Bingo, but you're clapping!

> 🎵 From Janet Carney, Aimee Ornstein, Pam
> Valente, and forty-six hundred others including
> yourself, your friends, and all your camp-mates.
> And Bingo was his name . . .

Diane Taub of Plainfield, New Jersey, says:
"I'm not sure, but I think we then did the
same thing in reverse. For example, the next
verse was the same as the next to last one
written . . . clap–clap–clap–clap–O. And then
we went on until we spelled out the entire
name—B–I–N–G–O—again." On that basis,
she and her friends could have gone on indefinitely and driven the camp and the coun-
selors crazy! But it's a good song.

Three Chartreuse Buzzards

This is sung to the tune of "Three Blind Mice."

Three Chartreuse Buzzards,
Three Chartreuse Buzzards
Sitting on a fence.
(spoken) Oh, look, one has flown A-way!
　　　　Isn't that A shame?

Two Chartreuse Buzzards,
Two Chartreuse Buzzards
Sitting on a fence.
(spoken) Oh, look, one has flown A-way!
　　　　Isn't that A shame?

One Chartreuse Buzzard,
One Chartreuse Buzzard
Sitting on a fence.
(spoken) Oh, look, one has flown A-way!
　　　　Isn't that A shame?

No Chartreuse Buzzards,
No Chartreuse Buzzards
Sitting on a fence.
(spoken) Oh, look, one has RE-turned!
　　　　Let us RE-joice!

One Chartreuse Buzzard,
One Chartreuse Buzzard
Sitting on a fence.
(spoken) Oh, look, one has RE-turned!
        Let us RE-joice!

Two Chartreuse Buzzards,
Two Chartreuse Buzzards
Sitting on a fence.
(spoken) Oh, look, one has RE-turned!
        Let us RE-joice!

Three Chartreuse Buzzards,
Three Chartreuse Buzzards
Sitting on a fence.
(spoken) Oh, look, one has flown A-way!
        Isn't that A shame?

And so on until you're tired.

Deborah Rodock, Canton, Ohio, from Camp
Tippecanoe, Ohio

The C Y O, the C Y O
Day Camp's the best, Day Camp's the best,
The very best, the very best
Of all the rest, of all the rest,
The C Y O Day Camp's the best,
The very best of all the rest.

We go on hikes, we go on hikes
When the weather is nice, when the weather
  is nice,
And we catch toads, and we catch toads
Along the road, along the road.
We go on hikes when the weather is nice,
And we catch toads along the road.

We go to arts, we go to arts
And crafts each day, and crafts each day
To paint or draw, to paint or draw
Or play with clay, or play with clay,
We go to arts and crafts each day
To paint or draw or play with clay.

And then we swim, and then we swim
Around the rim, around the rim
To keep in trim, to keep in trim
And full of vim, and full of vim,
And then we swim around the rim
To keep in trim and full of vim.
To keep in trim and full of vim.

And then it's time, and then it's time
For all of us, for all of us
To board the bus, to board the bus
Without much fuss, without much fuss,
And then it's time for all of us
To board the bus without much fuss.

      Janet Carney, Trenton, New Jersey

100 Bottles of Beer on the Wall

100 bottles of beer on the wall,
100 bottles of beer,
If one of those bottles should happen to fall,
99 bottles of beer on the wall.

99 bottles of beer on the wall,
99 bottles of beer,
If one of those bottles should happen to fall,
98 bottles of beer on the wall.

98 bottles of beer on the wall,
98 bottles of beer,
If one of those bottles should happen to fall,
97 bottles of beer on the wall.

And so on: 96, 95, 94, all the way down to

1 bottle of beer on the wall,
1 bottle of beer,
If that one bottle should happen to fall,
NO bottles of beer on the wall!

Sharon Weber, Brooklyn, New York, says that this song was sung at camp during long trips on the bus, or until youngsters voices and lungs gave out.

*Way up in the sky
the little birds fly,
While down in the nest
the little birds rest...
With a wing left
and a right,
We'll let the dear birdies
sleep the night...*

Wake up Song

"Our counselor at camp
used to wake us up
singing this song:

Way up in the sky
The little birds fly,
While down in the nest
The little birds rest—
With a wing on the left
And a wing on the right,
We'll let the dear birdies
Sleep all through the night.

Shhhh—They're SLEEPING! (screamed)

The sun comes up,
The dew falls away,
"Good morning, good morning,"
The little birds say.

Judy Deutsch, Syosset, New York. I imagine that with that scream many youngsters rolled out of bed wondering what had hit them. However, the day lay ahead, and the red team probably beat the blue, and a package of cookies came from home, and there might even be a letter from the boyfriend. But that scream . . . so early in the morning . . . brrrr!

Good Morning

Good morning to you,
Good morning to you.
You look very drowsy,
In fact you look lousy.
Is that any way
To start out the day?

> Amy Singer, Barrington, Rhode Island, from a camp counselor at East Brewster, Massachusetts. (I would say, offhand, that camp counselors are a fairly rough lot—or at least pretend to be—early in the morning. Actually they're probably quite nice by ten o'clock.)

Three Jolly Fishermen

There were three jolly fishermen,
There were three jolly fishermen,
Fisher-fisher-men-men-men,
Fisher-fisher-men-men-men,
There were three jolly fishermen.

The first one's name was Ja-a-cob,
The first one's name was Ja-a-cob,
Ja-a-cob-cob-cob,
Ja-a-cob-cob-cob,
The first one's name was Ja-a-cob.

The second one's name was I-Isaac,
The second one's name was I-Isaac,
I-I-saac-saac-saac,
I-I-saac-saac-saac,
The second one's name was I-Isaac.

The third one's name was Abraham,
The third one's name was Abraham,
Abra-Abra-ham-ham,
Abra-Abra-ham-ham,
The third one's name was Abraham.

They all went down to Amster-shush!
They all went down to Amster-shush!
Amster–Amster–shush–shush–shush,
Amster–Amster–shush–shush–shush,
They all went down to Amster-shush!

You must not say that naughty word!
You must not say that naughty word!
Naughty-naughty-word-word-word!
Naughty-naughty-word-word-word!
You must not say that naughty word!

I'm gonna say it anyway!
I'm gonna say it anyway!
Any-any-way-way-way!
Any-any-way-way-way!
I'm gonna say it anyway!

They all went down to Amster-DAM!
They all went down to Amster-DAM!
Amster–Amster–DAM–DAM–DAM!
Amster–Amster–DAM–DAM–DAM!
They all went down to Amster-DAM!!!

Brenda Lebowitz, New Rochelle, New York,
from summer camp

284

Stay on the Sunnyside

Stay on the sunnyside, always on the
    sunnyside,
Stay on the sunnyside of life—doo, do,
    doodo, dododo.
You will feel no pain as we drive you
    insane, so
Stay on the sunnyside of life.

> Knock, knock.
> Who's there?
> Ether.
> Ether who?
> Ether bunny. Ohh . . .

Stay on the sunnyside, always on the
    sunnyside,
Stay on the sunnyside of life—doo, do,
    doodo, dododo.
You will feel no pain as we drive you
    insane, so
Stay on the sunnyside of life.

> Knock, knock.
> Who's there?
> Nuther.
> Nuther who?
> Nuther ether bunny.   Ohh . . .

Stay on the sunnyside, always on the
    sunnyside,
Stay on the sunnyside of life—doo, do,
    doodo, dododo.
You will feel no pain as we drive you
    insane, so
Stay on the sunnyside of life.

> Knock, knock.
> Who's there?
> Still.
> Still who?
> Still another ether bunny. Ohh . . .   .

Stay on the sunnyside, always on the
   sunnyside,
Stay on the sunnyside of life—doo, do,
   doodo, dododo.
You will feel no pain as we drive you
   insane, so
Stay on the sunnyside of life.

   Knock, knock.
   Who's there?
   Car.
   Car who?
   Car come and run over all the ether
   bunnies. Ohh . . .

Stay on the sunnyside, always on the
   sunnyside,
Stay on the sunnyside of life—doo, do,
   doodo, dododo.
You will feel no pain as we drive you
   insane, so
Stay on the sunnyside of life.

   Knock, knock.
   Who's there?
   Boo.
   Boo who?
   Don't cry, ether bunny will be back next
   year. Ohh . . .

Stay on the sunnyside, always on the
   sunnyside,
Stay on the sunnyside of life—doo, do,
   doodo, dododo.
You will feel no pain as we drive you
   insane, so
Stay on the sunnyside of life.

   Bobbi Berman, Baltimore, Maryland. (Have
   you driven your mother and father completely
   off their rockers? They won't send you to camp
   next year! But it's fun.)

Little Rabbit Foo-Foo

Little rabbit Foo-Foo hopping through the
    forest,
Scooping up the field mice and tapping
    them over the head.
Down came the Good Fairy, and she said,
"Little rabbit Foo-Foo, I don't like your
    attitude,
Scooping up the field mice and tapping
    them over the head.
I'll give you three chances to be good,
And then I'll turn you into an ugly old
    goon."

So the next day little rabbit Foo-Foo
    hopping through the forest,
Scooping up the field mice and tapping
    them over the head.
Down came the Good Fairy, and she said,
"Little rabbit Foo-Foo, I don't like your
    attitude,
Scooping up the field mice and tapping
    them over the head.
I'll give you two chances to be good,
And then I'll turn you into an ugly old
    goon."

So the next day little rabbit Foo-Foo
    hopping through the forest,
Scooping up the field mice and tapping
    them over the head.
Down came the Good Fairy, and she said,
"Little rabbit Foo-Foo, I don't like your
    attitude,
Scooping up the field mice and tapping
    them over the head,

I'll give you one chance to be good,
And then I'll turn you into an ugly old
    goon."

So the next day little rabbit Foo-Foo
    hopping through the forest,
Scooping up the field mice and tapping
    them over the head.
Down came the Good Fairy, and she said,
"Little rabbit Foo-Foo, I gave you three
    chances to be good,
But you weren't!"
So she waved her magic wand at him and
"Poof!"—
Little rabbit Foo-Foo was an ugly old goon
    for the rest of his life.

Now the moral is this: "Hare today, goon
tomorrow."

> 🥕 Denise Miness, Baldwin, New York. "I
> learned this song from another counselor the
> first summer I worked as a counselor at Camp
> Costigan, Long Island. I have sung it to my
> groups every summer since, and have found
> that it is always the favorite."

Eat and Sleep

Eat and sleep and eat and sleep
And eat and sleep and eat and sleep,
Eat and sleep and eat and sleep,
And for a change I sleep and eat!

> Susan Cohen (from her aunt, Clair Cylinder) Philadelphia, Pennsylvania, the 1960s

A Nothing Song

Nothing, nothing, nothing, nothing,
Nothing all day long,
Nothing, nothing, nothing, nothing,
How do you like my nothing song?

Second verse, same as the first,
Can't get better, so it's gonna get worse.

Nothing, nothing, nothing, nothing,
Nothing all day long,
Nothing, nothing, nothing, nothing,
How do you like my nothing song?

Third verse, same as the first,
Can't get better, so it's gonna get worse.

Nothing, nothing, nothing, nothing . . . .

And so on indefinitely until you reach the:

Hundredth verse, same as the first,
Can't get better, so it's gonna get worse.

Nothing, nothing, nothing, nothing . . . .

Time for a coke, isn't it?

> Aimee J. Ornstein, Long Beach, New York

Welcome Song

We welcome you to Camp Allen,
We're mighty glad you're here,
We'll send the air reverberating
With a mighty cheer.
We'll wash you in,
We'll wash you out,
We'll stuff your mouth with sauerkraut!
Hail, hail, the garbage pail,
And you're welcomed to Camp Allen!

Denise Miness (from campers at Camp Allen), Oceanside, New York. And after that charming welcome, what then?

We Are Crazy

This is a song which is something like a combination of a couple we've had before. And that is folklore—nothing is fixed or permanent. Folklore changes always. You probably will say that this song is "wrong" and that the "correct" way to say or sing it is something that you know—and not this. OK. You're right, but so is Mark Kurtz and this song. He's right, too.

We are crazy, we are crazy,
We are nuts, we are nuts,
Happy little morons, happy little morons,
That is us, that is us.

Nothing, nothing, nothing, nothing,
We do nothing all day long.
We do absolutely nothing . . .
That's the end of my nothing song.

🖐 Mark Kurtz, Old Bridge, New Jersey

Do You Want to Play Calliope?

This can be played with four, but is probably better with eight youngsters. All of you are alternately popping up and down making the background music of a carnival or circus. It is a sing-song, chanting uproar.

(the first two persons):	Um-pa-pa, um-pa-pa, um-pa-pa
(the second two):	Um-tweet-tweet, um-tweet-tweet, um-tweet-tweet
(the third two):	Hammer-chisel-chisel, hammer-chisel-chisel, hammer-chisel-chisel
(the fourth two):	Peanuts-popcorn, peanuts-popcorn, peanuts-popcorn, peanuts-popcorn

And keep going and going until you have it down to crazy perfection!

  Janet Carney, Trenton, New Jersey

Davenport

D–A–V–E–N–P–O–R–T spells davenport,
  davenport,
That's the only decent kind of love seat,
  love seat.
The man who made it must have been a
  heartbeat, heartbeat.
D–A–V–E–N–P–O–R–T you see . . . .
It's a hug, and a squeeze, and an
Oh!, _____, please!
It's Davenport for me!

         🎜 Diane Taub, Plainfield, New Jersey

The Oyster Song

Once I ordered an oyster stew,
Alone tee hee alone,
One little oyster looked at me,
Alone tee hee alone.
He winked and blinked and smiled at me,
"In many a stew I've been," said he,
"But don't tell the cook that you saw me,"
Alone tee hee alone.

"Maybe I'll go to (Camp A. U.),"
Alone tee hee alone,
"Maybe I'll live in a dorm alone,"
Alone tee hee alone,
"And if a girl should smile at me,
I'll wink and blink and smile with glee,
For at (Camp A. U.) one cannot be alone,"
Alone tee hee alone.

John Jacob Jingleheimer Schmidt

John Jacob Jingleheimer Schmidt,
His name is my name, too,
And whenever we go out,
The people always shout,
"There goes John Jacob Jingleheimer
Schmidt!"
DA DA DA DA DA DA DA

Repeat this again and again. This song is
begun on a very loud pitch, and each con-
secutive time it is sung it gets softer and
softer, until the very last time when it is
barely audible—and then the DA DA DA DA
DA DA DA is screamed!

Brenda Lebowitz, New Rochelle, New York,
and Nancy Alessi, Connecticut

I Know a Camp that Is Co-Ed

I know a camp that is co-ed,
At least that's what the owners said,
Alas, alack, we were misled,
Romance just hasn't got a chance,
Not Here!

The moon shines down so big and bright,
Two lovers kiss into the night,
And then we see a sorry sight,
O. D.'s are searching through the trees
For Us!

We've seen in films and movies that a
    summer love
Can be exciting, inviting, and everlasting,
    too,
But in the movies flashlights never ever
    interrupt
When Marlon Brando and his girl begin to
    woo.

It isn't just that we can't bust from this
    Frus-tra-tion.
Oh, Farrington, please pity us,
We've found some boys to love and trust,
But since you're making such a fuss,
Romance just hasn't got a chance
    NOT HERE!

> Diane Taub, Plainfield, New Jersey. "A
> song we wrote at Camp Farrington, 1966."

I Want to Go Home

This is a universal cry and would seem to come from every girl's camp up and down the eastern seaboard. It is not too seriously meant, and yet there is, of course, home-sickness.

Three more weeks of frustration,
Then we go to the station,
Back to civilization.
I want to go home Right Now!
I want to go home,
I want to go home,
Back to mother and father,
Back to sister and brother,
Back to boyfriend and lover,
I want to go home!

    Janet Carney, Trenton, New Jersey

CHEERS AND YELLS

**2–4–6–8
Who do we appreciate?
The bus driver, the bus driver,
Yeah! The bus driver!**

> 🌿 Diane Mulbauer, Fairlawn, New Jersey.
> "The first summer I went to camp, we sang
> this every day when we arrived at camp."
> (Camp Belle)

**California oranges,
Texas cactus,
We play the red team
Just for practice!**

> 🌿 Karen Nichols, Brooklyn, New York. "This
> was a common cheer used during color war
> between the red and blue teams." (Camp
> Brookwood)

**Ashes to ashes,
Dust to dust,
We hate to beat you
But we must, we must!**

> 🌿 Sharon Nash, Washington, D.C. A cheer
> at McKinley High School.

I'm a raindrop, I'm a raindrop,
I'm a raindrop from the sky,
But I'd rather be a raindrop
Than a drip from Coyle High.

> 🖎 Veronica Casey, Taunton, Massachusetts.
> "This was sung to the tune of 'Clementine'
> at rallies when we played our big rival, Coyle
> High."

Rah Rah Ree,
Kick 'em in the knee!
Rah Rah Rass,
Kick 'em in the other knee!

> 🖎 Lee Hardgrove, Huntington, New York.
> From cheerleaders at Walt Whitman High
> School, Huntington, New York

We're on the warpath,
The warpath's hot,
We can't lose with the team we've got!
'Cause when you're up, you're up,
And when you're down, you're down,
But when you're up against us,
You're upside down!

> 🖎 Pamela Lewis, Oxon Hill, Maryland. From
> highschool cheerleaders.

Rhymes
and
Jingles
and
ODDS
and
ENDS

ALICE

"Alice, where are you going?"
"Up to take a bath."
Alice, with legs like toothpicks
And a neck like a giraffe,
Alice stepped in the bathtub.
Alice pulled out the plug.
"Alice, where are you going?"
"Glub, glub, glub!"

🌿 Collected by Jo Anne Kessler, from Alice
Braunstein of Corte Madero, California

TARZAN

"This is a rhyme that I chanted when I was
in grammar school."

Tarzan flying through the air,
Tarzan lost his underwear.
Tarzan said, "Me no care,
Jane will make me another pair."

Boy flying through the air,
Boy lost his underwear,
Boy said, "Me no care,
Jane will make me another pair."

Jane flying through the air,
Jane lost her underwear.
Jane said, "Me no care,
Tarzan like me better bare."

🌿 Ellen Fincke, Harrington Park, New Jersey

MARY, MARY

A variation on an old rhyme:

Mary, Mary, quite contrary,
How does your garden grow?
With silver bells and cockle shells
And one stinkin' petunia.

    ✿ Glen Feinberg, Yonkers, New York

HUMPTY DUMPTY

And another variation:

Humpty Dumpty sat on a wall,
Humpty Dumpty had a great fall.
All the King's horses and all the King's men
Had scrambled eggs for breakfast again!

    ✿ Janice Keidel, Arlington, Virginia

LITTLE MISS MUFFET

And still another:

Little Miss Muffet sat on a tuffet
Eating her curds and whey,
Along came a spider and sat down beside her,
And beat her to death with the spoon.

    ✿ Lee Sleininger, Florham Park, New Jersey

THE DUKE OF YORK

This is an old-timer, a very old-timer, but a good one to chant with friends.

The grand old Duke of York
He had ten thousand men,
He led them up to the top of the hill
And led them down again.
And when they're up, they're up,
And when they're down, they're down,
But when they're only halfway up
They're neither up nor down.

🖎 Remembered by Katherine McManus from her childhood at St. Thomas School, Binghamton, New York

EATING PEAS

I eat my peas with honey,
I've done it all my life:
It may seem kind of funny,
But it keeps them on my knife.

🖎 Collected by Audrey Lee, River Edge, New Jersey, from a five-year-old relative, Tracy Syatt, who recited it "much to everyone's surprise at the dinner table." It is an oldie but a goodie.

POOR ROBIN

The North wind doth blow,
And we shall have snow,
And what will poor Robin do then?
Poor thing.

He'll sit in the barn
And keep himself warm
And tuck his head under his wing.
Poor thing.

      🍃 From England, of course, but it came to
Veronica Casey, as sung to her by her grand-
mother in Taunton, Massachusetts, when
Veronica was a child. Nice?

SHORTIES

A chicken in the bread tray
Scratching out dough.
Granny, will your dog bite?
No, child, no.

    🍃 Traditional Kentucky

Fuzzy Wuzzy wuz a bear,
Fuzzy Wuzzy had no hair,
Fuzzy Wuzzy wusn't fuzzy,
Wuz he? Wuz he?

    🍃 Ellen Fincke, Harrington Park, New Jersey

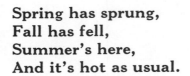

Spring has sprung,
Fall has fell,
Summer's here,
And it's hot as usual.

> Sharon Dill, Somerville, New Jersey

Spring has sprung,
The flowers has riz,
I wonder where
The birdies is?

> Judith Whipple, New York City

One shoe off,
One shoe on,
Diddle, diddle, dumpling,
My son John.

> Doris Labie, New York City, who learned this childhood rhyme from Barbara Friedman, Montclair, New Jersey

Little Betty Baker,
Her mother was a shaker,
But the more she shook her,
The more her wits forsook her.

> Sally Emrich, my wife, who heard it around about 1920 in Washington, D.C., and who still loves it

We ain't what we want to be.
And we ain't what we're going to be,
But we ain't what we wuz.

> 🖎 Collected by Susan Niemiera, Perth Amboy,
> New Jersey, from Diane Sofield of Miami,
> Florida.

I'm a little tea pot, short and stout
Here is my handle, and here is my spout,
When I get all steamed up, then I shout:
"Tip me over and pour me out!"

> 🖎 Diane Taub, Plainfield, New Jersey

NOW I AM A BIG BOY

When I was a little boy
About so high,
Mama took a little stick
And made me cry.

Now I am a big boy,
Mama can't do it;
Papa takes a big stick
And tends right to it.

> 🖎 Traditional North Carolina

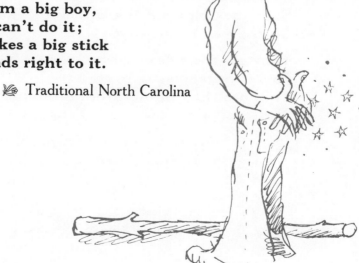

THE ASTRONAUTS

The astronauts went up in space,
Up in space, up in space.
The astronauts went up in space
On the way to the moon.

They took off from the launching pad,
Launching pad, launching pad.
They took off from the launching pad,
On the way to the moon.

They ate their dinner from plastic bags,
Plastic bags, plastic bags,
They ate their dinner from plastic bags,
And washed it down with Tang.

Paula Huston, age 5, brought home from school, Seneca, Maryland

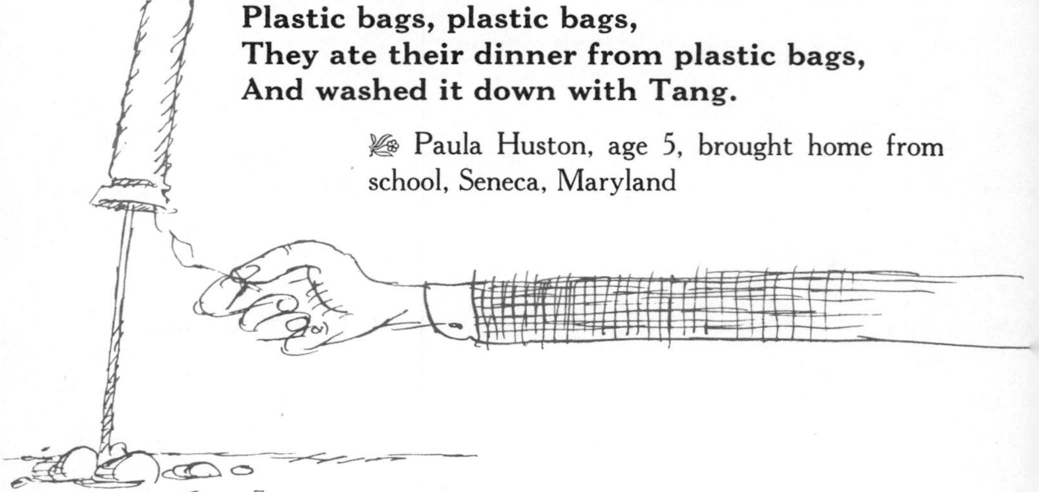

ON TOP OF SPAGHETTI

To the tune of "Old Smoky"

On top of spaghetti
All covered with cheese
I lost my poor meatball
When somebody sneezed.
It rolled off the table
And onto the floor;
The last time I saw it,
It rolled out of the door.
A truck ran it over,
It died the next day,
I honor my meatball
On Memorial Day.

🐝 Picked up by Martrice Green at the Madison Elementary School, Washington, D.C., 1960.

Anatomy of a Disaster:
1 SNEEZE
2 MEAT-BALL
TABLE
3
N
DOOR (WAY OUT)
4
FLOOR
0   1"

On top of spaghetti
All covered with cheese
I lost my poor meatball
When somebody sneezed.
It rolled off the table
And onto the floor;
The last time I saw it,
It rolled out of the door.
It rolled into the garden
And under a bush
And then my poor meatball
Was nothing but mush.

🐝 Brought from school by Paula Huston, age 5, Seneca, Maryland; also from Nancy Volz who knew it as a youngster in Syosset, New York.

LINCOLN

Lincoln, Lincoln,
I've been thinkn',
What in the heck
Have you been drinkin'?
Is it whiskey, is it wine?
Oh, my gosh, it's turpentine!

This was turned in by so many youngsters
and students that I could put at least fifty
names of contributors. It baffles me. Why
is it so popular? It makes no sense whatever. From Lincoln to drinking to turpentine! It is possibly because it makes no real
sense that it is popular. But if anyone can
supply me with a good reason for its exist-
ence, I'll send him/her a five pound box of
Velati's caramels—and they are the best in
the world.

EERIE STUFF

In **THE HODGEPODGE BOOK** (p. 164) there
was a scary rhyme beginning:

Did you ever think as the hearse rolls by
That some day in it you will lie . . . .

Now try this one from Carol Behm, Dearborn
Heights, Michigan:

Never laugh when a witch goes by,
For you may be the next to die.
She'll wrap you up in a big white sheet
And throw you under about six feet.
You're alright for about a week,
But then your casket begins to leak.
Your eyes fall in,
And your teeth fall out,
The ants play pinochle on your snout.
Your stomach turns a mushy green . . . .
   Oh, shucks, I forgot my spoon!

You don't want that strawberry milkshake
right now? Why ever not?

MR. TURNER AND HIS TURNIP

**Mr. Turner had a turnip.
And it grew behind the barn.
And it grew and it grew
And grew and grew
Until it couldn't grow any longer.
Then Mr. Turner pulled it up
And put it in the cellar.**

✍ Linda Coleman (from her mother), Boston, Massachusetts

ISN'T IT FUNNY?

**Isn't it funny that night falls,
But day breaks?**

✍ Martrice Green, Washington, D.C. Quite interesting thought. Acquired by Martrice from an 11-year old.

BARBER, BARBER

Barber, barber,
Shave a pig.
How many hairs will make a wig?
Four-and-twenty, that's enough.
Give the good barber a pinch of snuff.

> From England, of course, but here from Christie Leighton and "a friend" in Minneapolis, Minnesota

THAT OLD RIVER AGAIN!

With an M and an I and an S-S-I
And an ippy and a pippy,
Spells MISSISSIPPI.

> Rhonda Madow (from her mother), Marblehead, Massachusetts

CAN SHORT PEOPLE SPELL?

On a school bulletin board one person wrote:
  Short People Can't Spell
Another student came along and underneath
that statement replied:
  Yes They Ken!

> Carolyn Peace, Melville, New York

LULLABY

Rock-a-rock a baby,
Mommy is a lady,
Daddy is a gentleman
Who buys the baby candy.

> Amy Singer, from her aunt in Barrington,
> Rhode Island

CLAP HANDS

When the baby is a little older:

Clap hands, clap hands
Till daddy comes home;
Daddy's got money,
But mommy's got none.

> Meryl Markowitz, Oceanside, New York

SO HELP ME, THE TRUTH!

You may well have heard this at camp, and
I've had it given to me by half a dozen students and youngsters. It's not to be recited
at table and some of your mothers may go
straight through the roof, but I'll bet that
most of them go off chuckling afterward:

You can pick your nose,
And you can pick your friends,
But you can't pick your friend's nose!

> Mitchell Stein, Lisa Moss, Lois Murray,
> and a batch of others. It's all yours. Take it
> away!

WORK

"Work fascinates me. I can watch it for hours."

   🌿 Lee Hardgrove, Huntington, New York, who heard this from his father, but I've also heard it elsewhere—and you, too, maybe.

GIGGLE DUST

When someone is laughing uncontrollably or giggling her head off:
 "You must have swallowed giggle dust!"

   🌿 Barbara Zeller (from her mother), Hillside, New Jersey

WE HAD THE BEST OF FUN

On Saturdays we had the best of fun,
We played Hop Scotch and Run, Sheep, Run,
Frog in the Meadow and Pull Away,
And anything else we wanted to play.
And after we'd played and played and played,
We had pink straws in our lemonade.
I can see it all, it's such a dream,
And all the Saturdays had ice cream.

> 🐌 Linda Colemen, from her mother, Boston,
> Massachusetts

Write 7 7 3 4
  on a piece of paper
    and hope
      when you turn it upside down that you
      will never go there

315

POLKA-DOTS

You know this one. When you see a lady wearing a polka-dot dress, say quickly:

Money, money, come to me
Before the day is through.
I spy polka-dots,
And polka-dots spy me.

You will receive money.

> 🌿 According to Kathie and Charles Friedley, Sussex, New Jersey, you will. How much? Two dimes? Maybe she will be wearing only a polka-dot scarf. A nickel?

CIRCULAR SONG

This endless song (make up an easy tune) will
drive your father right up the wall. Be careful!

1 Found a peanut
   Found a peanut
   Found a peanut just now.
   Just now I found a peanut,
   Found a peanut just now.

2 Cracked it open
   Cracked it open
   Cracked it open just now.
   Just now I cracked it open,
   Cracked it open just now.

3 It was rotten

4 Ate it anyway

5 Got sick

6 Called a doctor

7 He came too late

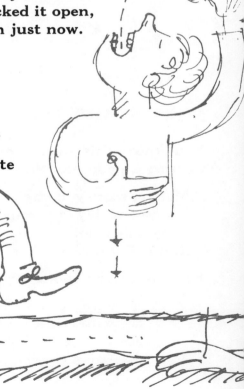

8   I died

9   Went to Heaven

10 Saw St. Peter

11 Kicked me out

12 Down to Hell

13 Saw the Devil

14 Let me in
    Let me in
    Let me in just now.
    Just now he let me in,
    Let me in just now.

15 Found a peanut
    Found a peanut
    Found a peanut just now.
    Just now I found a peanut,
    Found a peanut just now . . . .

❧ From Peter Broderick, South Freeport, Maine, 1956. Contributed by Shelley Broderick, American University, 1973

COW JOKE

We are in the Wild West—Arizona, New Mexico, or Texas, or somewhere out yonder.

City Lady: Look at that bunch of cows.
Cowboy: No, herd.
City Lady: Heard of what?
Cowboy: Herd of cows.
City Lady: Sure, I've heard of cows!
Cowboy: No, a cow herd.
City Lady: What do I care what a cow heard? I've got no secrets from a cow!

🌿 Martrice Green, Washington, D.C., who heard this from a 10-year-old boy. It's a goody. Total misunderstanding by the City Lady.

ENDLESS RIGAMAROLE

1st person: Pete and Repeat were walking across the street. Pete ran away. Who was left?
2nd person: Repeat.
1st person: Pete and Repeat were walking across the street. Pete ran away. Who was left?
2nd person: Repeat.
And so on endlessly.

🌿 Debra Skopczynski, remembered from her childhood, Dearborn Heights, Michigan

THREE SLIGHTLY DEAF OLD LADIES

Three slightly deaf old ladies were taking a cruise together. As they were taking a walk around the deck, the first old lady said, "Windy, isn't it?" The second old lady replied, "No. I think it's Thursday." The third old lady said, "I'm thirsty, too. Let's go get a drink." So they all went inside to get a drink.

    🌿 Mary Campbell, Chevy Chase, Maryland. "I heard and loved this as a child in Chevy Chase. It seems to delight children, as I've told it to mine, and I've heard them repeat it many times to their friends."

AT TABLE

Immediately after grace at table, in order to break the silence, my grandfather would say: "Go easy on the butter. It's 69 cents a pound."

> Debra Skopczynski, Dearborn Heights, Michigan, in the 1960s.

and also from Debra:

My stomach is so empty, I think the first thing I eat is going to echo.

and

I think my stomach is devouring itself.

and heard by her from Marc Rosenberg, an American University student from Philadelphia, about a young man who was probably fairly clumsy:

His problem is that he tiptoes in wooden shoes.

TABLE CODES

These are "secret" codes within a family. They are used when there are guests for lunch-eon or dinner.

When the supply of food at the table is run-ning low and the guests still seem hungry, the mother or father may quietly say "FHB," which means: "Family Hold Back."

> 🖎 Sharon Dill, Somerville, New Jersey

And the opposite, from my own childhood, "MIK," standing for, "More In the Kitchen." So—help yourself to more mashed potatoes and gravy!

A GENTLE BLESSING OR THANKS

We got bread,
We got meat,
Now all you little children
Begin to eat.

> 🖎 Melinda McFarlin, Fort Lauderdale, Flor-ida, says that when she was a youngster in Montezuma, Iowa, her father "often used to say this before the evening meal."

322

TACT

Just as in the secret table codes within a family, there are other "codes" to tell a person that something is wrong with his or her clothing—without letting the whole world know what you're talking about. Here are a few. You may know others.

R. S. V. P. means "Ribbon Showing Very Plainly." This is used to tell a friend discreetly that her slip or bra straps are showing.

"It's snowing down South" means that your slip is showing.

"You're slipping." This also means that your slip is showing.

"You're crying." This is to let you know that your stockings are bagging around your ankles.

X Y Z—This stands for "Examine Your Zipper," and it is not embarrassing to say this to a youngster whose zipper happens to be undone.

These are from students of mine at American University: Ronnie Aronchick, Sharon Weber, Mary Campbell, and Shelley Broderick, all of whom collected them from grade schoolers—perhaps from one of you.

WEATHER

In **THE HODGEPODGE BOOK**, there was a whole section on weatherlore. Here are just a few more items to add to those.

Thunder is God stuttering.

    🌿 Marie Kisner, San Antonio, Texas

When I was a child, I thought that snow was dandruff coming out of God's head whenever He scratched it.

    🌿 Nancy Gendler, South Hampstead, New York

If you wash your hair, it will rain the next day.

    🌿 Doris Indyke, Rockville Center, New York

But Cathy Robertson claims it will rain the same day: It never fails to rain the day you wash your hair.

    🌿 Cathy Robertson, Oyster Bay, New York

**If you want rain, wash your car.
If you want drought, plant a new lawn.**

> Ellen Aszkenas, Fair Lawn, New Jersey, who heard those from her grandfather

If you step on an ant, it's going to rain. If you step on a whole bunch of ants, it's going to pour! (If you want a nice day, or if you're going on a picnic or to the ball game, don't step on ants!)

If the birds are singing, it's going to rain.

> Both from Janet Disken, New Haven, Connecticut

It's 100° in the shade, and there ain't no shade!

(You can be sure that's from Texas, and it is.)

> 🖎 Marie Kisner, San Antonio, Texas, and told to her by her father

Out in the West they say that when the wind blows from the north in January and February, "the only thing between the North Pole and Texas is barbed wire."

> 🖎 Jean Lambert, Athens, Pennsylvania

Arise at five in the morning on New Year's day. If the wind is from the north, it will be a good fruit year.

> 🖎 Judith Warrington heard that from her aunt in the Cumberland Mountains, Tennessee

If there is a full moon out, and the night is clear and cold, frost will come.

> 🖎 Marianne Hollister, Wheaton, Maryland, learned from her grandparents

TRAFFIC FOR 3rd GRADERS

And it won't hurt you to know them and teach them!

Hippity Hop

Hippity Hop, Hippity Hop,
Green says Go
And Red says Stop!
That is how I always know
When to Stop and when to Go.

Look Out

Look out, look out before you cross the street,
Look up, look down to see what you can see.
And if there are no cars in sight,
Walk and walk with all your might,
Walk, walk, walk,
Walk with all your might.

(Never, never run!)

Go, but look each way

Traffic Lights

Red light, red light, what do I say?
I say stop and stop right away.
Yellow light, yellow light, what do I mean?
I mean wait till the light turns green.
Green light, green light, what do I say?
I say Go, but *look each way.*
Thank you, thank you, Red, Yellow, and Green,
Now I know what the traffic lights mean.

🌿 Margie Kovens Fisher, Bethesda, Maryland

Let the Ball Roll

Let the ball roll,
Let the ball roll,
No matter where it may go,
Let the ball roll,
Let the ball roll,
It has to stop sometime, you know!

And after it's stopped, you can go get it after looking up and down the street. But if you chase it without looking, then someone who is not looking also in an automobile might hurt you very badly. Always be careful. Always look.

🌿 Barbara Zeller, Hillside, New Jersey

TIME

In the Spring clocks are moved forward one hour and in the Fall back one hour to adjust to Daylight Saving and then return to Standard Time. Usually people are confused about this and forget whether to move clocks backward or forward in the Spring and Fall. They get into arguments and often call their newspapers or radio stations to settle the dispute. But there is a very simple way of remembering. It is this:

Spring forward!
Fall back!

QUITE CRAZY

Two crazy but also very true proverbs:

Laugh, and the world laughs with you. Snore, and you sleep alone!

Be true to your teeth, or they will be false to you!

    🐌 Maureen Mintz, Roslyn, New York, and learned from her father

CLEAN UNDERWEAR

Many mothers and grandmothers have advised their daughters to "wear clean underwear" for the following reason:

"Always wear clean underwear in case something happens and you end up in the hospital."

> 🌿 Vickie Harrowe (from her mother), Bronx, New York

"Always wear clean, untorn underwear in case you are (God forbid!) in an accident and a stranger sees you undressed for an examination."

> 🌿 Rhonda Madow (from her mother), Marblehead, Massachusetts

"Always wear clean underwear in case you get hit by a truck."

> 🌿 Arlene Eisenberg (from her grandmother), Flushing, New York

AN OATH

Instead of saying simply "Cross my heart and hope to die," here is a stronger oath to swear two or more people to secrecy. This is especially for secrecy. Secrecy only.

Earth and water and fire and air,
I solemnly promise, I solemnly swear
Not a look, not a word, not a sound to declare,
Earth and water and fire and air.

 ✎ Ronnie Aronchick, Bradley Beach, New Jersey

TONGUE TWISTERS

If two witches were watching two watches, which witch was watching which watch?

> 🐝 Sheri Miller, Hinds County, Mississippi, and gathered by George Boswell, University, Mississippi

**Sixty-seven smiling sisters
Sitting in the sunshine singing songs
And chewing cheese.**

> 🐝 Vicky Dann, Westport, Connecticut, and learned from her mother, New York City

**Beautiful blue banlon,
Beautiful blue banlon,
Beautiful blue banlon . . .**

> 🐝 John Coursen, Princeton, New Jersey. "Banlon" is a synthetic fabric.

Aluminum linoleum

Unique New York

    🖙 Jo Anne Kessler, Brooklyn, New York

Ann Anteater ate Andy Alligator's apples, and angry Andy Alligator ate Ann.

    🖙 Martrice Green, Washington, D.C.

T. T. F. N.

Instead of saying "Good-by" as a farewell expression to someone, say: "T. T. F. N."— which is an abbreviation for "Ta, ta, for now."

    🖙 Melinda McFarlin, Fort Lauderdale, Florida

The chief sources for the SATOR charm are: Mary A. A. Dawson, *Puzzles and Oddities*, New York, 1876; Thomas Rogers Forbes, *The Midwife and Witch*, New Haven, 1966 (with excellent bibliography); Jean Marques-Rivière, *Amulettes, Talismans et Pantacles dans les Traditions Orientales et Occidentales*, Paris, 1938; Liselotte Hansmann and Lenz Kriss-Rettenbeck, *Amulett und Talisman, Erscheiningsform und Geschichte*, Munich, 1966 (heavily and beautifully illustrated); John George Hohman, *Pow-Wows, or, Long Lost Friend. A Collection of Mysterious and Invaluable Arts and Remedies for Man As Well As Animals*, Westminster, Maryland, 1855, and Harrisburg, Pennsylvania, 1856 (thousands of copies have been sold since then, and the SATOR charm is still in use in Pennsylvania German country). For Magic Squares the chief sources include Forbes and Marques-Rivière as cited above, and E. A. W. Budge, *Amulets and Talismans*, 1930, with reprint edition New York (Macmillan) 1970.

With the exception of the section on Magic Squares and SATOR and the section on "Wishes" (letters from youngsters around the country), virtually everything else in *Whim-Wham* has been contributed from the collections of my students at American University. I am especially grateful to Marcy Devine of Tolland, Connecticut, who did three superb papers on "Autograph Album Verse," and from which I have drawn for a goodly number of the "Tricky" or designed items. To all those named in the text I express my appreciation and thanks. To the many not named and who also deserved inclusion, my apologies. I wish particularly to thank also Nancy Alessi for tracking down the home towns of the contributors of the many items, and Joy Huston for the fine typing of the manuscript. Their assistance made the completion of the work measurably easier than it would otherwise have been.

DATE DUE
